Centro Cooks
A Celebration of the Seasons

Centro Cooks

A Celebration of the Seasons

Barbara Prevedello

A RUSSET BOOK

RANDOM HOUSE OF CANADA

TORONTO

Published in 1996 by Random House of Canada Limited, Toronto

Canadian Cataloguing in Publication Data

Prevedello, Barbara

  Centro Cooks: a celebration of the seasons

ISBN 0-679-30823-7

1. Cookery-Ontario-Toronto. 2. Cookery, Canadian.

I. Centro (Restaurant). II. Title

TX715.6.P74 1996 641.5′09713′541 C96-930341-6

Project Management: Paula Chabanais & Associates Limited / Russet Books

Editor: Beverley Endersby

Food Testing and Styling: Dana McCauley

Art Direction and Design: Peter Maher

Photography: Richard Swiecki

Printed in China

♥

FOR
FRANCO

Contents

WINTER

SPRING

Acknowledgements

The production of *Centro Cooks* took place, for several months, without Franco's knowledge. During that time, while researching recipes, writing methods, attending photo sessions, and creating this book, I was well aware that its scope would have been limited without the input of several talented and caring professionals, whom I thank for indulging my clandestine plan, often under challenging circumstances: Paula Chabanais, for her unwavering vision of the book's direction and execution; Dana McCauley, for upholding the integrity of the Centro food; and Richard Swiecki and Peter Maher, for their creative talents and flexible agendas.

The staff at Centro made a large contribution to this book and share the credit for its completion —Marc Thuet and Tony Longo, both of whom brought a whole new meaning to the term "silent partners" while keeping my secret. Marc contributed his culinary creativity with the seasonal highlight menus. Tony, whose love of and expertise in wine, selected the perfect accompaniments to each recipe. Leslie House contributed her translation skills and meticulous attention to detail, and Armando Mano contributed himself for three days as a "cast of one" at the photo sessions.

Although this book was a surprise to Franco, it reflects his personality as clearly as his presence is felt in the restaurant.

Finally, these acknowledgements would not be complete without sincere thanks to the loyal clientele, who continue to be the largest part of our success story.

Introduction

Centro Cooks: A Celebration of the Seasons is a tribute to Franco Prevedello, whose vision and determination created a fast-paced, uptown eatery which has successfully met the challenges of time and change and which, after ten years, continues to be an innovative contributor to Toronto's food scene.

In January 1986, Franco secured the property at 2472 Yonge Street, and a new concept for the 10,000-square-foot space took shape. Almost two years later, on November 5, 1987, concept became reality when the beautifully sculptured glass doors were opened to reveal a gracious and magnificent interior featuring eighteen-foot high columns; oversize photographs of Franco's home town, Asolo, in northern Italy; tables laid with crisp white linen and shining crystal; imported, custom-made furniture, satin-finished wooden floors, and handsome Italian wine cabinets that displayed bottles with mysterious labels, reverently lit by a single overhead beam. The sense of warmth and magic was enjoyed by a throng of first-nighters, and continues to excite and entice all those who arrive for a dining experience at Centro.

In the first few weeks, 2,000 books of matches were handed out; the laundry service washed 1,000 napkins a day; 200 pounds of Parmesan cheese were grated over perfect *al dente* pasta; and the wood-burning pizza ovens consumed a cord of wood every few days. Liquor was flowing, and orders for mineral water were scant.

Today, the restaurant continues to run at capacity six nights a week: the kitchen produces 300 to 400 meals a day; 120 cases of wine are consumed every week; and mineral water is consumed by the case.

At the heart of the restaurant's success is the quality and integrity of the food. The high standards of presentation and innovative cuisine that were set on opening night, continue to be upheld.

Centro Cooks offers a selection of the restaurant's classic and modern dishes. The classics include Cream of Pumpkin Soup, Zuppa di Pesce, Veal Chop, and Rack of Lamb with Herb Crust. Modern dishes, such as Tender Vegetable Salad in Saffron Vinaigrette, reflect the spectacular variety of salad greens available today, and will delight the palate attuned to vegetarian fare.

In the highlight menus that introduce each season, Chef Marc has created four, sumptuous five-course meals that utilize the freshest products available in a season and showcase evolving styles in food presentation.

The wine cellar of 40,000 bottles of primarily Italian wines has been expanded over the years to include New World wines and French labels. The wines recommended as the best accompaniments to these recipes have been carefully selected to reflect the sophisticated international wine tastes of our clientele.

All the recipes have been tested for the domestic kitchen. The chef's suggestions for serving and presentation will help the home cook treat friends and family to a restaurant-style culinary experience with confidence.

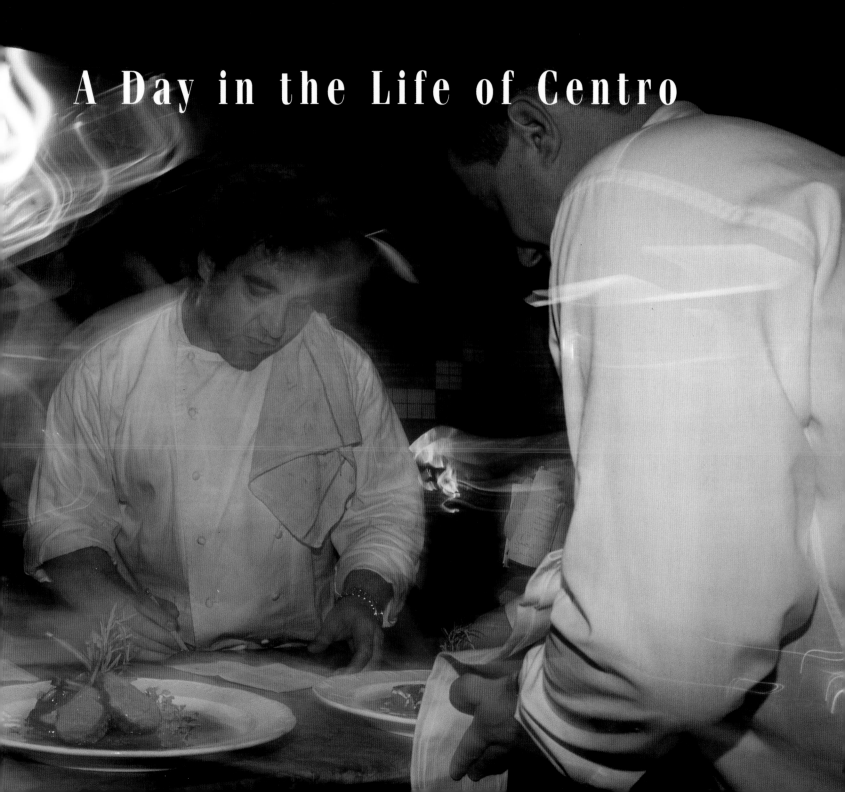

A Day in the Life of Centro

8:15 a.m. Arrive at the back door, where deliveries abandoned by drivers unwilling to wait for a receiver are piled high. Shove bags of bread away from the entrance, struggle with the key in the lock, climb over bags, trying not to squash a loaf, step inside. The phone is ringing, as usual. Flick on the lights, stagger up the stairs to key-in the alarm code. Keys fall down the stairwell. Rush down to retrieve them; stagger back upstairs to the alarm panel. The phone persists. Lock on office door sticks but gives in to a swift kick. Enter, and dive for the telephone: "Good morning, Centro" is met with a dial tone.

8:35 a.m. Back outside to retrieve bread. First call is to the supplier—words are exchanged. Line 2 lights up: "Good morning, Centro. How can I help you?" Persistent knocking at the front door turns out to be a film crew who have booked the Centro dining room as the location for an interview with a current celebrity. Twelve people enter, carrying a truckload of equipment.

8:45 a.m. The cleaning staff arrive! The phone rings—a forgotten credit card; the owner will come by this morning on his way to the airport. A cruise through the walk-in refrigerators produces nothing that appeals for morning fare. Raw carrots and onions, the odd pail of beef broth or peeled potatoes in a bucket of water, or the remains of the tray of garnishing herbs.

9:20 a.m. The back door opens and bangs closed with a delivery and expectations of something to eat… Milk, a wholesome start… Not long after, twenty cases of mineral water. First cook arrives. The look on his face as he

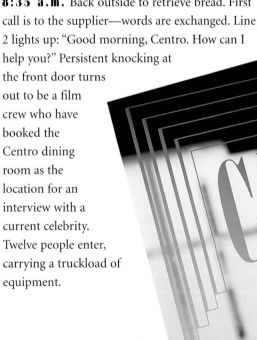

staggers toward the coffee machine tells the tale of the late night before. The phone continues to ring—reservations, information about the current menu, a forgotten briefcase under table 45. Menus are faxed, gift certificates issued, and parties booked.

10:30 a.m. Filming in the dining room has reached a critical point. The crew demands that the phones be turned off during the taping. Centro's life-line is put on hold at 20-minute intervals throughout the morning. When they are allowed to ring, all three lines light up and demand attention: directions to the restaurant from Mississauga, a request for information regarding this evening's specials.

12:15 p.m. The manager arrives to help with the phones and reservations. The kitchen staff straggle in and head towards the coffee machine. Deliveries continue to be announced by the piercing beep of trucks as they inch their way up the lane to the back door. Wine and liquor deliveries arrive and are stored away to be inventoried and requisitioned for the bartenders.

1:00 p.m. On the way to the bank, stop by the party store to order a dozen birthday balloons, requested by the party who reserved the private room, to be picked up later. A waiter calls to ask for his schedule time: he forgot to check before leaving town yesterday, and now he's in London

and can't get to work before 6:00 p.m.

2:15 p.m. With the back lane completely blocked by delivery trucks, the owner of the property next door wants to park in his space, without further delay, and is honking his horn to make his point.

3:00 p.m. The first shift of waiters arrives, passing directly to the coffee machine; the film crew shows no sign of finishing by 3:30, as promised.

the private party in the Cantina room. The chef's wife and kids stop by for a visit with Daddy, who distributes biscotti all round.

5:00 p.m. Waiters hustle from the change room, adjusting their ties as they head for the meeting where the sous-chef will explain tonight's specials in detail. The front door of the restaurant is opened and it's like a curtain going up: everyone takes a deep breath.

5:30 p.m. Behind the sparkle of the dining room, the kitchen is producing like a well-oiled machine. The head chef takes up his position at the "pass," where a last touch of garnish or additional sauce is added before dishes are presented to the customers. Orders come from the dining room to the impact printer in the kitchen, with loud and persistent clacking; the chef peels off the paper and begins to conduct. "Ordering, table 4: two soup, one carpaccio, one smoked salmon, one scallop, one pasta." Cooks move about the kitchen without missing a beat, preparing for the call of the chef, "Pick-up table 4." The kitchen takes on the din of an auction house; the noise is deafening and the heat intense; thirty gas burners going full blast; the mesquite barbecue-grill coals are glowing; the red-hot pizza oven is devouring hardwood like a bonfire; and the twenty-gallon stock pot bubbles rigorously in a corner, making that perfect beef broth for tomorrow.

4:00 p.m. A waiter, stuck in traffic on the 401 from Brampton, has paid one dollar to a driver in the next lane for the use of his mobile phone to inform the manager of his dilemma. More service staff arrive. The side stand is cleared of dirty coffee cups and spoons; the film crew are, at long last, packing up their equipment.

4:30 p.m. Perched on milk crates, in the back lane, the staff are taking a break before the night service begins; a meat supplier returns with forgotten items from an earlier delivery, and a wine salesman arrives with the special order for

coals in the pizza oven are raked over to cool.

12:00 p.m. The dining room empties; a few customers head down to the wine bar for a nightcap; the mood has mellowed; whispers of conversations are heard throughout the room; the chef joins a table for a nightcap; the last customers have no more demands.

9:30 p.m. Just when a party of twelve arrives, the computer crashes. Communication from dining room to kitchen has been severed; the pace accelerates, nerves are frayed, adrenaline is flowing.

11:00 p.m. A few more parties arrive for an after-theatre supper; the dessert cook is meticulously writing a birthday greeting on the cake ordered for the party in the Cantina.

11:30 p.m. Customers are relaxing over their port or grappa; the kitchen clean-up crew are washing the last of the pots and pans; garbage is hauled to the front street for pick-up, and the

1:00 a.m. The clean-up continues. After the garbage truck has passed, the street and front walk are hosed down. These late-night hours are spent in reflection on the day's labours, with renewed anticipation of what tomorrow will bring. Tomorrow we will change the soup and add the chef's new special. Tomorrow, for the party of thirty-five., we will offer the new vintage Barolo being released by the liquor board in the morning. Tomorrow will be another day at Centro, unlike any that has gone before.

Summer

CHEF'S MENU

*Ragoût of Lobster and
Rabbit Fillet in Summer
Truffle Essence
page 18*

*Trio of Tataki Marc Thuet
page 25*

*Melon Consommé
page 99*

*Medallions of Veal
with Cèpcs and Chive Jus
page 32*

*Soufflé of Ontario
Strawberries
page 33*

RECOMMENDED WINES:

Tocai Friulano
Mario Schiopetto
Friuli

Chardonnay
Patz & Hall
Napa Valley

Muscadet de Sèvre-et-Maine
Joseph Drouard,
Loire

Ragoût of Lobster and Rabbit Fillet in Summer Truffle Essence

SERVES 4

2 cooked lobsters (1 lb/500 g each)
½ cup (125 mL) unsalted butter, cubed
2 cloves garlic
1 sprig each, rosemary and thyme
4 rabbit fillets (3 oz/80 g each)

4 oz (125 g) black trumpet or seasonal mushrooms
¼ cup (50 mL) finely chopped shallots or onions
½ cup (125 mL) Sauternes or other sweet wine
2 cups (500 mL) lobster jus (p. 102)

2 tbsp (30 mL) 35% cream
1 tsp (5 mL) truffle oil
⅔ cup (75 mL) blanched garden peas
8 slices of black truffle
chervil sprigs

Cut lobster tails into 3 equal pieces and remove meat from the shell. Remove claw meat and leave whole, reserving the shells for the jus.

In a large skillet over low heat, melt 2 tbsp (30 mL) butter. Add garlic, rosemary, and thyme, and cook for about 5 minutes, until garlic is translucent. Increase the heat; add the 4 rabbit fillets and cook over medium-high heat for 3 minutes per side, or until medium rare, basting constantly. Remove from pan and reserve.

In the same pan, cook the trumpet mushrooms for 2–3 minutes until browned. Remove and reserve with the rabbit.

Using the same pan, sauté the shallots over medium heat until translucent, but not browned.

Deglaze the pan with the Sauternes, and cook for about 3 minutes to reduce to ½ original volume. Add the lobster jus; boil for 10 minutes until reduced to about 1 cup (250 mL). Whisk in the cream and the remaining butter, bit by bit. Or, if preferred, transfer the reduced stock and cream mixture to a blender and blend in the butter, a little at a time, at high speed, until a foamy sauce is formed. Pour back into the saucepan, and add the truffle oil, lobster tails, and peas.

TO SERVE: Cut the 4 fillets of rabbit into equal-sized slices. Place equal portions of the black trumpet mushrooms on each of 4 dinner plates; top with the lobster ragoût, the rabbit fillets, and the truffle slices. Garnish with sprigs of chervil, additional mushrooms, and reserved lobster claws.

✓ excellent

RECOMMENDED WINES:
Sauvignon del Collio
Az. Agr. Venica
Friuli

Chardonnay
G.E. Vallania
Emilia Romagna

Corbulino Bianco
Az. Agr. Tobia Scarpa
Veneto

Insalata Caprese with Roasted Red Peppers

SERVES 4

4 red peppers, halved and seeded
2 tsp (10 mL) extra virgin
   olive oil
2 beefsteak tomatoes
8 oz (250 g) buffalo mozzarella
   or bocconcini cheese

basil leaves
cracked black pepper

DRESSING:
¼ cup (50 mL) red wine vinegar
2 tbsp (30 mL) basil, chopped

¼ tsp (1 mL) each, salt and
   pepper
pinch of sugar
½ cup (125 mL) extra virgin
   olive oil

TO PREPARE THE DRESSING: Whisk together vinegar, basil, salt, pepper, and sugar in a small bowl. Slowly add oil, in a steady stream, whisking constantly. Reserve.

TO PREPARE THE PEPPERS: Rub skins with oil and place under a broiler for 7–8 minutes, turning until blackened and blistered. Remove from broiler and place in a tightly covered bowl for 15 minutes, until cool enough to handle. Using fingertips, slip off the charred skins and discard. Cut the skinned peppers into slices and reserve.

TO ASSEMBLE: Slice tomatoes and cheese thinly and arrange with peppers and basil leaves in an attractive manner on serving platter. Drizzle with dressing and sprinkle with cracked pepper.

Tender Vegetable Salad in Saffron Vinaigrette

SERVES 4

VINAIGRETTE:
¼ cup (50 mL) warm water
2 tsp (10 mL) white wine vinegar
1 clove garlic, minced
1 pinch each, saffron, granulated
  sugar, and cayenne
¼ cup (50 mL) extra virgin
  olive oil

SALAD:
4 small beets or 1 large beet
12 snow peas
1 bulb fennel
20 French green beans
8 each, yellow and red cherry
  tomatoes
4 small zucchini

16 green asparagus stalks
1 tbsp (15 mL) butter
12 chanterelles or other firm
  mushrooms
salt and pepper
fresh chervil and salad greens
  to garnish

TO PREPARE THE VINAIGRETTE: Whisk together warm water, vinegar, garlic, saffron, sugar, and cayenne in a small bowl. Slowly add oil, in a steady stream, whisking constantly. Set aside.

TO PREPARE THE VEGETABLES: *Beets:* Wash, peel, and cut stalk 1 inch (2.5 cm) above the bulb. *Snow Peas:* Remove top and tail, and slice diagonally. *Fennel:* Wash and remove the fibrous outer layer, and slice thinly. *French Beans:* Remove top and tail. *Cherry Tomatoes:* Wash and pat dry carefully. *Zucchini:* Wash and cut off the stems. *Asparagus:* If the stalks are big, peel them; if not, just wash them. Use only top 3 inches (7.5 cm) of the tip. *Chanterelles:* Trim the base of the stalks. Wash quickly in cold water; pat dry.

TO COOK THE VEGETABLES: Bring to a boil 8 cups (2 L) of water with 2 tbsp (30 mL) of salt. Blanch fennel for 1 minute; add beans, asparagus, and zucchini, and boil for 1 minute; add snow peas and cook for 1 minute longer. Drain in a colander and plunge into ice water for 1 minute. Drain again. Season with salt and pepper.

TO COOK THE MUSHROOMS: In a skillet over high heat, melt butter; add chanterelles and sauté for 2 minutes, or until slightly softened and golden brown. Season to taste with salt and pepper. Set aside.

TO DRESS: Place the blanched vegetables and tomatoes in a large mixing bowl. Add about ½ of the vinaigrette and toss lightly.

TO ASSEMBLE: In the centre of 4 individual plates, arrange the vegetables in an attractive manner. Place the mushrooms over the vegetables, and sprinkle with the remaining vinaigrette. Garnish with the chervil and other salad greens.

Vodka Gazpacho

S E R V E S   4

RECOMMENDED WINES:

Fiano Di Avellino P.L.D.
Mastroberardino
Campania

Sauvignon Blanc
Byron
Santa Barbara

Rully
Domaine de la Renard
Burgundy

1 can tomatoes (14 oz/543 mL) or 2 medium, fresh, ripe tomatoes, skinned and coarsely chopped

1 cup (250 mL) diced and peeled English cucumber

½ cup (125 mL) each, chopped red and yellow peppers

¼ cup (50 mL) chopped onion

1 clove garlic, peeled and finely chopped

1 tbsp (15 mL) minced chili pepper or ¼ tsp (1 mL) Tabasco

¼ cup (50 mL) chicken stock *(p. 100)*

2 tbsp (30 mL) extra virgin olive oil

2 tbsp (30 mL) chopped fresh basil leaves

1 tsp (5 mL) chopped fresh oregano leaves

½ tsp (2 mL) each, salt and pepper

¼ cup (50 mL) vodka

In a blender or food processor combine tomatoes, cucumber, peppers, onion, garlic, and chili pepper. Purée 30–40 seconds, until well combined. Add stock, olive oil, basil, oregano, salt, and pepper, and blend for another minute, until smooth and thick.

May be refrigerated at this point for up to 12 hours. Before serving, adjust seasoning and add the vodka.

SUGGESTED GARNISHES: Julienne of 3 fresh basil leaves; finely chopped yellow pepper; or garlic croutons.

Trio of Tataki Marc Thuet

Riesling
Hengst
Josmeyer
Alsace

Vintage Tunina
Az. Agr. Jermann
Friuli

Chardonnay Reserve
Cameron
Oregon

2 oz (50 g) lamb tenderloin, 1½–2 inch (4–5 cm) in diameter

2 tbsp (30 mL) each, granulated sugar and salt

5 oz (150 g) each, tuna and swordfish loin, 1½–2 inch (4–5 cm) in diameter

1 tbsp (15 mL) tamari *(p. 109)*

2 sweet yellow peppers, chopped

2 tbsp (30 mL) sesame seeds, roasted

1 tbsp (15 mL) pink peppercorns, crushed

2 tbsp (30 mL) pickled ginger juice

¼ cup (50 mL) coriander oil (recipe below)

1 tbsp (15 mL) mirin *(p. 108)*

½ tbsp (7 mL) sesame oil

2 cups (500 mL) frisée or other curly lettuce

salt and pepper

CORIANDER OIL:

½ cup (125 mL) parsley

2 cups (500 mL) coriander

2 cups (500 mL) extra virgin olive oil

In a bowl, toss lamb tenderloin with 1 tbsp (15 mL) sugar and 1 tbsp (15 mL) salt and the tamari. Cover and marinate for 30 minutes. Stir together remaining salt and sugar; turn tuna and swordfish in mixture to coat; cover and marinate in refrigerator for 30 minutes.

Meanwhile, liquefy yellow peppers in a food processor or blender. Press purée through sieve into a small saucepan. Over medium heat, simmer essence for about 25 minutes, until reduced to ¼ cup (50 mL); allow to cool.

Rinse lamb, swordfish, and tuna; pat dry. Roll tuna in the roasted sesame seeds, and roll the swordfish loin in the crushed peppercorns, until evenly coated.

In a cast-iron frying pan over high heat, sear the swordfish, tuna, and lamb loins, one at a time, on all sides until they are blackened all over. Cool to room temperature.

Slice each loin into 8 equal round pieces.

CORIANDER OIL: Blanch the parsley and coriander in boiling salted water for 1 minute. Remove, and plunge into ice water. Drain well. Squeeze out excess water; process in a blender with the olive oil for approximately 4 minutes. Strain through a fine-mesh sieve or cheesecloth before using. Decant if necessary.

Whisk ginger juice and 2 tbsp (30 mL) coriander oil into ½ of the pepper essence. In a mixing bowl, whisk mirin and sesame oil; toss with frisée; season with salt and pepper to taste.

TO SERVE: Arrange alternating pieces of lamb, swordfish, and tuna tataki in a circle, slightly overlapping, in the centre of each of 4 chilled dinner plates. In the centre of each circle, place an equal amount of the frisée salad. Drizzle the plate with the remaining ½ of pepper essence, the remaining coriander oil, and the ginger mixture.

RECOMMENDED WINES:

Taurasi
Az. Vin. Mastroberardino
Campania

Zinfandel Nalle
Dry Creek Valley

Bric Mileui
Matteo Ascheri
Piedmont

Penne all'Arrabbiata

SERVES 4 – 6

¼ cup (50 mL) extra virgin
    olive oil
2 cans Italian plum tomatoes,
    drained (28 oz/796 mL each)

½ tsp (2 mL) hot pepper flakes
1 lb (500 g) penne
salt and freshly ground pepper, to
    taste

Parmesan cheese, freshly grated

Heat the oil in a saucepan over medium heat, add the tomatoes, and cook for 25 minutes, stirring often with a wooden spoon. Season to taste with salt and pepper.

Cool slightly, then pass the mixture through a food mill fitted with a fine disc (with the smallest holes), or a mesh sieve, into a second saucepan. Discard seeds. Return the tomato purée to medium heat, add the hot pepper flakes, and simmer for 15 minutes over low heat, until thick enough to coat the back of a spoon.

Bring a large pot of cold water to a boil; salt the water and add the pasta. Cook until *al dente* (9–12 minutes). Drain and transfer to a warm serving bowl. Toss with the sauce, adding salt and pepper to taste. Serve with freshly grated Parmesan cheese.

Zuppa di Pesce

SERVES 6

RECOMMENDED WINES:

Chardonnay
Az. Agr. Maculan
Veneto

Sancerre
Domaine Vacheron
Loire

Sauvignon Blanc
Geyser Peak
Sonoma

ROUILLE (a garnish traditionally accompanying bouillabaisse):
1 jalapeño pepper, seeded and roasted
1 sweet red pepper, seeded and roasted
4 garlic cloves, peeled and chopped
½ cup (125 mL) lemon juice
2 egg yolks
1 tbsp (15 mL) Dijon mustard
1 cup (250 mL) extra virgin olive oil
1 cold baked potato

pinch of salt and pepper and cayenne
melba toast

LOBSTER:
½ onion, peeled
½ carrot, peeled
2 bay leaves
1 sprig each, basil and rosemary
1 lemon, halved
2 cups (500 mL) white vinegar
1 lobster (1 lb/500 g)

FISH:
2 tbsp (30 mL) extra virgin olive oil
1 onion, chopped
3 cloves garlic, minced
2 tbsp (30 mL) finely chopped lemon grass
4 cups (1 L) fish stock (p. 100)
4 oz (125 g) each red snapper, grouper, and salmon (cut into 1-inch/2.5-cm pieces)
20 mussels
4 each shrimp and scallops, cleaned

TO PREPARE THE ROUILLE: In a blender or food processor, purée peppers, garlic, lemon juice, egg yolks, and mustard until smooth; with motor running, drizzle in olive oil.

Remove and discard the skin from the baked potato and put potato through a ricer, or mash until smooth; combine with the pepper mixture until blended well. Season with salt, pepper, and cayenne. Set aside.

TO PREPARE THE LOBSTER: Bring a large stock pot of salted water to a boil. Add the onion, carrot, bay leaves, basil, rosemary, lemon halves, and vinegar. Immerse the lobster in the water, for 5–7 minutes until red. Cool and cut in half;

discard the head, crack the claw shells, and set aside.

TO PREPARE THE FISH: In the olive oil, sauté the chopped onion, garlic, and lemon grass. Cook, stirring often, until onions are very soft. Stir in the fish stock and bring to a boil. Reduce heat to medium; add fish and mussels, immersing completely in stock. Reduce heat to simmer; add shrimp and scallops and the lobster pieces. Simmer for another minute. Set aside.

TO SERVE: Place the cooked fish and shellfish in an attractive manner in 4 large soup plates. With a ladle, spoon the broth on top of the fish. Garnish each serving with melba toast topped with rouille.

Fillet of Nova Scotia Salmon with Tarragon Sauce

SERVES 4

4 sprigs tarragon
2 tbsp (30 mL) extra virgin
   olive oil
4 salmon fillets (about 8 oz/250 g
   each)
2 cups (500 mL) fish stock
   (p. 100)
½ cup (125 mL) shallots or

onions, finely chopped
1 sprig fresh thyme
1 bay leaf
½ cup (125 mL) white wine
1 cup (250 mL) lightly packed
   watercress and spinach leaves
¼ cup (50 mL) chervil or parsley
   leaves

½ cup (125 mL) cold butter
½ tsp (2 mL) each, salt and
   pepper
¼ cup (50 mL) salmon roe or
   steelhead roe

Remove tarragon leaves from stems and chop stems finely. Reserve leaves.

In a mixture of the olive oil and chopped tarragon stems, toss the salmon, turning to coat. Cover and refrigerate for 2 hours.

Bring the fish stock, shallots, thyme, and bay leaf to a boil in a saucepan over medium-high heat; add the white wine and simmer for 20 minutes, or until reduced slightly. Strain the liquid through a fine sieve and discard the herbs and shallots.

Blanch the reserved tarragon leaves, watercress, spinach, and chervil in boiling salted water for 1 minute, or until bright green; drain, then cool under cold running water for 1 minute. Squeeze dry and chop fine. Add chopped herb mixture to the fish-stock and simmer for 5 minutes to exchange the flavours.

Cut the cold butter into small pieces and whisk, piece by piece, into the simmering stock. Season with ¼ tsp (1 mL) each, salt and pepper; keep warm.

Remove the salmon fillets from the marinade, and season with the remaining salt and pepper. Grill or broil until the salmon is cooked through— about 7–10 minutes.

TO SERVE: Spoon the tarragon sauce onto 4 warmed plates, and place a salmon fillet in the centre of each. Top each fillet with a dollop of the roe. Serve with seasonal vegetables or pasta.

Rack of Lamb with Herb Crust

SERVES 4

RECOMMENDED WINES:

Château Palmer
Margaux
Bordeaux

Cabernet Sauvignon
Cask 23 Stag's Leap
Napa Valley

Tignanello
Piero Antinori
Tuscany

2 racks lamb, French-cut
1 tbsp (15 mL) extra virgin olive oil
½ cup (125 mL) fresh bread crumbs
1 tsp (5 mL) each, chopped fresh thyme, rosemary, oregano, and parsley

½ tsp (2 mL) each, salt and pepper
1 clove garlic, minced
1 tbsp (15 mL) Dijon mustard
¼ cup (50 mL) shallots, finely chopped

2 cloves garlic, peeled and sliced
1 bay leaf
sprigs rosemary
1 cup (250 mL) lamb jus *(p.103)*
2 tbsp (30 mL) butter, cubed
salt and pepper

Season the meat with salt and pepper. In a roasting pan, heat the olive oil over medium-high heat. Sear the lamb on both sides. Place lamb on a wire rack in the same roasting pan and roast in a 400 F (200 C) oven for 15 minutes.

In a large mixing bowl, stir together bread crumbs, chopped herbs, minced garlic, salt, and pepper.

Remove lamb from oven and spread mustard over the meaty sides and both ends of the racks. Place racks, one at a time, in the crumb mixture; spoon crumbs evenly over mustard-coated surfaces. Return racks to roasting pan and place under a hot broiler for 2–3 minutes, or until golden brown. Place lamb on heated platter, tent with foil, and leave to rest.

In the same roasting pan, over medium heat, add shallots, sliced garlic, bay leaf, and 1 sprig of the rosemary. Cook, stirring often, for 5 minutes or until shallots are softened. Add the lamb jus and bring to a boil. Simmer rapidly for 5 minutes, or until reduced to about ½ cup (125 mL). Gently whisk in the cubed butter. Adjust seasoning to taste. Strain through a fine-mesh sieve.

TO SERVE: Carve the racks into individual chops and place on 4 dinner plates. Drizzle the sauce around the meat. Garnish with sprigs of rosemary.

Medallions of Veal with Cèpes and Chive Jus

Serves 4

¼ cup (50 mL) each, Madeira and port
1¼ cup (300 mL) veal jus *(p. 102)*
¼ cup (50 mL) butter, cubed
2 tbsp (30 mL) chopped fresh chives
2 tbsp (30 mL) butter

2 tbsp (30 mL) finely chopped shallots
1 clove garlic, minced
½ lb (250 g) cèpes or other mushrooms
8 medallions, veal tenderloin (3 oz/80 g each)

salt and pepper to taste
1 tbsp (15 mL) extra virgin olive oil

TO PREPARE THE CHIVE JUS: In a small saucepan, bring to a boil the Madeira and port and cook until reduced to ½ original volume. Add veal jus and return to a boil; reduce to about ½ cup (125 mL). Decrease heat to medium low; add cubed butter, bit by bit, whisking until sauce is smooth and thick. Add chives, and season to taste. Set aside.

TO PREPARE THE CÈPES: In a skillet over medium heat, melt 1 tbsp (15 mL) of the butter; stir in shallots and garlic. Cook, stirring often until softened, about 5 minutes. Increase heat to high, and add mushrooms. Cook for 3–4 minutes until well browned, stirring often. Set aside.

TO PREPARE THE VEAL: Season the veal medallions with salt and pepper. Heat the olive oil and remaining 1 tbsp (15 mL) butter in a large, clean skillet. Over medium-high heat, cook medallions for 3 minutes per side, or until golden brown but still slightly pink in the centre.

TO SERVE: In the centre of each of 4 heated dinner plates, arrange the veal medallions; top with the cèpes. Drizzle liberally with chive jus. Garnish with chopped chives and seasonal vegetables.

Soufflé of Ontario Strawberries

SERVES 4

RECOMMENDED WINES:

*Pol Roger Rosé
Champagne*

*Opere Trevigiane Villa Sandi
Veneto*

*Piper Sonoma Brut
Sonoma*

PASTRY CREAM:
¼ cup (50 mL) lemon juice
¼ cup (50 mL) 35% cream
3 egg yolks, beaten
⅓ cup (75 mL) granulated sugar
2 tbsp (30 mL) all purpose flour

1 tbsp (15 mL) finely chopped
   lemon zest

MERINGUE:
3 egg whites
½ cup (125 mL) granulated sugar
4 strawberries, hulled and
   quartered
icing sugar

TO PREPARE THE PASTRY CREAM: Heat the lemon juice and cream in a saucepan over medium-high heat until steamy. In a bowl, whisk egg yolks and sugar to a ribbony consistency—about 1 minute. Stir in flour and zest. Whisking constantly, gradually incorporate hot lemon–cream mixture, return mixture to saucepan and set over medium heat for 3 minutes, whisking constantly until thickened. Remove from heat and cool to room temperature.

TO PREPARE THE MERINGUE: Using an electric mixer, beat egg whites until frothy. Gradually add the sugar, beating constantly. Continue beating for 1½ –2 minutes or until mixture is thick and glossy and holds its shape. Fold a small amount of meringue into the cooled pastry cream. Gently fold in the remaining meringue until combined but still streaky. Carefully transfer mixture to a pastry bag. Pipe a donut-shaped ring of batter into 4 well-buttered 4 inch (10 cm) oven-proof soufflé dishes. Place 4 strawberry quarters in each hole; pipe in enough batter to cover the strawberries and fill dish to the ⅔ mark. Place in freezer for 1 hour. May be completed to this point and kept frozen for up to 2 days.

Bake in a 400 F (200 C) oven for 10–12 minutes until puffed and lightly browned. Dust with icing sugar, and serve immediately.

CHEF'S SUGGESTION: Serve with fruit sauces, such as strawberry or orange, or a rhubarb compote.

Caramelized Lemon Tart

SERVES 6

CRUST:

2 cups (500 g) all-purpose flour

¾ cup (175 mL) icing sugar, sifted

1 tbsp (15 mL) finely chopped lemon zest

seeds from 1 vanilla bean

½ cup (125 mL) cold butter, diced

1 egg, beaten

LEMON FILLING:

½ cup (125 mL) 35% cream

4 eggs

1 egg yolk

1 cup (250 mL) granulated sugar

1 tbsp (15 mL) finely chopped lemon zest

⅔ cup (150 mL) lemon juice

1 tsp (5 mL) icing sugar

RECOMMENDED WINES:

*Riesling
Late Harvest
Cave Spring Cellars
Ontario*

*Malvasia Della Lipari
Carlo Hauner
Sicily*

*Gewürztraminer
Grains Nobles
Lucient Albrecht
Alsace*

TO PREPARE THE CRUST: In a large bowl, stir together flour, icing sugar, lemon zest, and seeds from vanilla bean. Cut in butter, using two knives, until mixture resembles coarse oatmeal. Add beaten egg and stir until mixture forms a ragged dough. Knead with hands until dough is smooth. Wrap in plastic and refrigerate 1 hour, or overnight.

Grease a 9-inch (23-cm) tart pan with removable bottom.

On a lightly floured surface, roll out the dough into a 13-inch (32-cm) circle. Place the dough into the tart pan, and cover with waxed paper. Refrigerate for 30 minutes.

TO PREPARE THE LEMON FILLING: In a small saucepan over medium heat, warm the whipping cream for 4–5 minutes, or until just beginning to steam. Cool slightly.

In a bowl, whisk the eggs and egg yolk. Gradually add sugar and lemon zest; continue whisking until fluffy and pale. Stir in lemon juice and warmed cream. Set aside.

Prick the crust all over with a fork. Line with waxed paper and cover surface with pie weights or dried beans. Ensure sides and base are weighted down.

Bake in preheated 350 F (180 C) oven for 10–12 minutes. Remove the beans/pie weights and the waxed paper, and return to oven for another 10 minutes, until crust is lightly browned.

Remove tart from oven. Reduce temperature to 250 F (120 C). Skim froth and bubbles from top of lemon filling; pour filling into tart shell. Return to oven, and bake 30 minutes, or until set.

TO SERVE: Sift icing sugar over the tart; place under broiler for 1–2 minutes, until caramelized or sugar is dissolved and golden brown.

CHEF'S SUGGESTION: Serve with sour-cream gelato or any fruit gelato.

Fall

CHEF'S MENU

Arctic Char with
Maple–Mustard Emulsion
and Coriander Oil
page 38

Suprême of Ontario Squab
with Quebec Foie Gras au
Jus Naturelle
page 44

Champagne Sorbet
page 99

Grouper à l'Alsacienne
with Braised Savoy Cabbage
page 49

Warm Truffle-Centre
Chocolate Ganache with
Poire William Coulis
page 53

Arctic Char with Maple-Mustard Emulsion and Coriander Oil

SERVES 4

RECOMMENDED WINES:

Beaujolais Moulin-a-Vent
Georges DuBoef
Burgundy

Chardonnay Reserve
Cave Spring Cellars Ontario

Chardonnay
Az. Agr. Regaleali
Sicily

CORIANDER OIL:

½ cup (125 mL) coriander

2 tbsp (30 mL) parsley

½ cup (125 mL) extra virgin
olive oil

MAPLE–MUSTARD EMULSION:

2 tbsp (30 mL) Dijon mustard

1 tbsp (15 mL) maple syrup

1 tbsp (15 mL) lemon juice

2 tsp (10 mL) sherry vinegar

¼ cup (50 mL) grapeseed or
vegetable oil

1 avocado, peeled, pitted, diced

2 tbsp (30 mL) lemon juice

1 mango, peeled, pitted, diced

2 tbsp (30 mL) coriander oil

2 plum tomatoes, seeded and
chopped

CHAR

6 oz (175 g) Arctic char fillet,
centre-cut, skinned, diced

2 tbsp (30 mL) finely chopped
shallots or onions

1 tsp (5 mL) each, mirin (*p. 108*)
and tamari (*p. 109*)

1 tbsp (15 mL) chopped chives

1 tsp (5 mL) each, salt and
pepper

1 cup frisée lettuce

4 tsp (20 mL) yellow caviar
(salmon roe, Arctic char roe,
whitefish roe)

4 oz (125 g) thinly sliced
Arctic char

CHEF'S SUGGESTION:
Salmon trout or salmon
may be substituted for
Arctic char.

TO PREPARE CORIANDER OIL: In a small pot of salted boiling water, blanch coriander and parsley for 30–60 seconds, until bright green. Remove and plunge into cold water. Drain well. Squeeze dry; place in blender and purée until smooth; pour in oil, blend for 3–4 minutes. Pass through a fine-mesh sieve or cheesecloth, and reserve. Decant if necessary before use.

TO PREPARE MAPLE–MUSTARD EMULSION: In a measuring cup or small bowl, whisk together mustard, maple syrup, lemon juice, and sherry vinegar. Still whisking, drizzle in oil. Reserve. In a small bowl, mix together avocado and lemon juice; add salt and pepper to taste. In another bowl, stir together mango and 1 tbsp (15 mL) coriander oil, and sprinkle with salt and pepper. In yet another bowl, mix tomatoes with remaining 1 tbsp (15 mL) coriander oil; sprinkle with salt and pepper. Toss the diced fish with shallots, mirin, tamari, chives; add salt and pepper to taste.

TO ASSEMBLE: Using a 3-inch (8-cm) round cookie cutter, build a tower in the centre of a dinner plate by packing ¼ of the avocado mixture into the ring, followed by ¼ of each of the mango, tomato, and fish mixtures. Pack lightly, and gently remove the ring. Towers may be made in advance, loosely covered, and refrigerated for an hour or more.

TO SERVE: Top each tower with an equal amounts of frisée; place dollops of caviar on top of each. Arrange Arctic char slices around tower; drizzle plate with coriander oil and maple–mustard emulsion.

RECOMMENDED WINES:

Pouilly Fumé
Henri Bourglois
Loire

Osborne Cream Sherry

Prato de Canzio
Az. Agr. Maculan
Veneto

Cream of Pumpkin Soup
served with Smoked Salmon

SERVES 4

4 cups (1 L) chicken stock
   (p. 100)
1 small pumpkin (about 8 cups
   /2 L peeled and diced
   pumpkin pulp)
1 tsp (5 mL) granulated sugar

¼ cup (50 mL) corn flour
¼ cup (50 mL) cold water
1 cup (250 mL) 35% cream
½ cup (125 mL) butter, cubed
4 oz (125 g) smoked salmon, cut
   in fine strips

2 tbsp (30 mL) 35% cream
1 tbsp (15 mL) chopped fresh
   chervil or parsley

In a saucepan, combine the chicken stock, diced pumpkin, and sugar. Bring the mixture to a boil, cover, and cook for 20 minutes, until pumpkin is soft.

Transfer mixture to a blender or food processor, and blend until smooth. Return mixture to saucepan and bring to a boil, stirring constantly. Remove from heat.

In a small bowl or cup, blend corn flour with the cold water. Whisk corn-flour mixture into soup until well combined. Return pan to heat, and simmer 1 minute. Whisk in 1 cup (250 mL) cream.

Transfer mixture to a blender; with motor running, add cubes of butter, a few at a time until it is all incorporated and soup is frothy and light. Strain through a mesh sieve; season to taste.

TO SERVE: Reheat without boiling. Place equal amounts of salmon in the bottom of 4 soup bowls; ladle in soup. Using a squirt bottle or large spoon, drizzle the remaining 2 tbsp (30 mL) cream on top in an attractive design. Sprinkle with chervil or parsley.

Château-Grillet
Neyret-Gachet
Rhône

Muscato di Andrea
Robert Pecota
Napa Valley

Pinot Bianco
Az. Agr. Paolo Caccese
Friuli

Salad of Wild Greens with Rabbit and Foie Gras in Lemon–Lime Dressing

SERVES 4

3 tsp (15 mL) each, butter and
  extra virgin olive oil
½ cup (125 mL) finely chopped
  shallots
½ tsp (2 mL) each, salt and
  pepper
4 boneless rabbit loins
4 escallopes of foie gras (3 oz/80
  g each)
¼ cup (50 mL) red wine

(i.e., Beaujolais)
½ cup (125 mL) game stock or
  chicken stock (p.100)
4 cups (1 L) mixed greens such as
  arugula, frisée, Boston lettuce,
  Belgian endive, radicchio
1 ripe peeled mango, thinly sliced
1 plum tomato, seeded and finely
  diced
salt and pepper

DRESSING:
1 lemon
1 lime
¼ cup (50 mL) extra virgin olive
  oil
1 tsp (5 mL) chopped shallots
fresh herbs: such as chives,
  chervil, and thyme
salt and pepper

CHEF'S SUGGESTION:
Chicken may be substituted
for rabbit; increase cooking
time by about 10–12
minutes.

TO PREPARE THE DRESSING: Squeeze the juice
of the lemon and lime into a small bowl. Slowly
add the olive oil and whisk until blended; add the
chopped shallots, the fresh herbs, and the salt and
pepper to taste.

TO PREPARE THE RABBIT AND FOIE GRAS: In a
skillet set over medium heat, melt 1 tsp (5 mL)
butter together with the olive oil. Add shallots and
cook, stirring often, for 2 minutes, until sizzling
and fragrant.

Season the rabbit loins and foie gras with salt and
pepper. Add rabbit to the skillet, and cook for 5
minutes until golden brown but still pink inside.
Remove from pan; tent with foil.

In the same pan, sear the escallopes of foie gras
for about 30 seconds on each side and remove
from pan; tent with foil.

Pour wine into skillet; increase heat to high and
cook bits for about 1 minute or until liquid is
reduced to about 2 tbsp (30 mL). Pour in stock
and continue cooking for about 5 minutes or until
reduced by ½. Whisk in remaining 2 tsp (10 mL)
butter to make jus thick and glossy.

TO ASSEMBLE: Toss the salad greens with the
dressing and reserve. Arrange the salad on 4 large
plates and garnish with 4–5 slices of ripe mango.
Cut the loin of rabbit into 2–3 slices and arrange
in an attractive manner. Arrange foie gras on and
around salad. Drizzle salad with the warm game
stock. Garnish plate with diced tomato.

Suprême of Ontario Squab with Quebec Foie Gras au Jus Naturelle

SERVES 4

RECOMMENDED WINES:

*Savigny-lès-Beaune
Girard-Vollot
Burgundy*

*Pinot Noir
Reserve
Inniskillin
Ontario*

*Primofiore
Az. Agr. Guiseppe Quintarelli
Veneto*

3 tbsp (45 mL) butter, cubed
¼ cup (50 mL) finely chopped shallots or onions
⅓ cup (75 mL) each, port and cognac
¾ cup (175 mL) squab jus (p. 103)
2 tbsp (30 mL) sesame oil
1 cup (250 mL) pineapple chunks

2 cups (500 mL) corn kernels
1 tsp (5 mL) chopped pickled ginger
¼ tsp (1 mL) each, salt and pepper
1 tbsp (15 mL) extra virgin olive oil
4 squab breasts (about 6 oz/75 g each)

2 tbsp (30 mL) chicken stock (p. 100)
1 tbsp (15 mL) mirin (p. 108)
8 cups (2 L) mixed greens, such as watercress, sorrel, frisée
8 oz (250 g) foie gras, sliced in 4
1 tbsp (15 mL) chervil or parsley, chopped

In saucepan over medium heat, melt 1 tbsp (15 mL) butter; add shallots and cook, stirring often, for 5 minutes, until softened. Pour in port and cognac; bring to a boil for 4–5 minutes until reduced to ½ cup (125 mL). Stir in squab jus; lower heat and simmer gently for 10 minutes, until reduced to ½ cup (125 mL). Whisk in remaining butter bit by bit; season to taste. Keep warm.

To a skillet over high heat, add 1 tbsp (15 mL) sesame oil, pineapple, and corn; cook, stirring, for 5 minutes, until golden. Add ginger, salt, and pepper; reserve.

In a roasting pan, with 1 tbsp (15 mL) olive oil over medium heat, cook squab breasts, skin side down, for 2 minutes, until browned. Place in a 400 F (200 C) oven for about 3 minutes, until breasts are cooked: pink in the middle, with crispy

dark skin. If using bone-in breasts, roast for about 7 minutes. Remove from pan and tent with foil. Let rest for 5 minutes.

TO PREPARE THE VEGETABLES: In another pan over high heat, heat remaining sesame oil with chicken stock and mirin. Add greens and stir for about 45 seconds, until wilted but still bright green.

TO PREPARE THE FOIE GRAS: In a hot dry pan, sauté seasoned foie gras quickly; 45 seconds on each side. Remove to a heated plate.

TO ASSEMBLE: On 4 individual hot plates, make 3 neat mounds of alternating wilted greens and foie gras. Place pineapple mixture in centre, and rest squab on greens. Drizzle sauce around and on the squab, and garnish with chervil and parsley.

Risotto con Funghi

SERVES 6

½ cup (125 mL) butter
1 small onion, sliced very thin
¾ lb (300 g) fresh porcini
    mushrooms or other fresh
    wild mushrooms

1 cup (250 g) dry white wine
3 cups (750 g) superfino arborio
    rice
7 cups (1.75 L) beef stock
    (p.101), warmed

¾ cup (175 mL) grated Parmesan
    cheese
2 tsp (10 mL) white truffle oil
    (optional)

RECOMMENDED WINES:

*Chinon Charles
Joguet
Loire*

*Gamay Beaujolais
Robert Pecota
Napa Valley*

*Barbera d'Alba
Az. Agr. Paolo Conterno
Piedmont*

Melt ½ the butter in a large, heavy pan and sauté the onion over medium heat for about 5 minutes, until soft and transparent, but not brown.

Clean the mushrooms and slice thinly. Add these to the pan and stir well. Increase heat to high; pour in the wine, and continue cooking 6–7 minutes, or until wine is almost evaporated. Remove onions and mushrooms from the pan; reserve.

Reduce heat to medium, add the rice, and cook for 3 minutes, or until rice begins to brown. Stir in ½ the warmed stock. Cook, stirring until the stock has been absorbed—about 5 minutes. Continue adding stock about ½ cup (125 mL) at a time, until all the stock has been absorbed and the rice is done to desired tenderness— approximately 20 minutes.

Remove from heat, add the remaining butter, Parmesan cheese, and truffle oil, and the reserved onions and mushrooms, stirring well. Cover the pan and leave the risotto to settle for 2–3 minutes before serving.

Duo of Canadian Venison in Pinot Noir and Blueberry Jus

S E R V E S   4

RECOMMENDED WINES:

Pinot Noir
Reserve
Robert Mondavi
Napa Valley

Amarone Classico
Az. Agr. Guiseppe Quintarelli
Veneto

Merlot
Vigna L'Apparita
Castello di Ama
Tuscany

2 shallots, finely chopped
2 tbsp (30 mL) extra virgin
  olive oil
½ cup (125 mL) Pinot Noir
¼ cup (50 mL) port
1 tbsp (15 mL) balsamic vinegar
⅔ cup (150 mL) venison jus
  (p. 103)

¼ cup (50 mL) cold butter,
  cubed
1 cup (250 mL) blueberries,
  cleaned
4 venison chops (4 oz/125 g
  each)
1 venison tenderloin (10–12 oz/
  300–375 g)

½ tsp (2 mL) salt and pepper
8 baby turnips, peeled and
  blanched
12 baby carrots, peeled and
  blanched
½ head Savoy cabbage, shredded

In a saucepan over high heat, sauté the shallots in 1 tbsp (15 mL) olive oil until golden. Add the Pinot Noir, port, and balsamic vinegar. Simmer for 5–7 minutes, or until reduced to ¼ cup (50 mL). Add the venison jus, and bring to a boil. Strain into a clean saucepan through a fine sieve. Bring to a simmer, and slowly whisk in ½ the cubes of butter. Add blueberries, and keep warm.

Season the venison chops on both sides with salt and pepper. In skillet set over medium-high heat, heat ½ tbsp oil; cook the chops, turning once, for 3 minutes, or until browned. Place in a 425 F (220 C) oven for 7–10 minutes, or until desired doneness is reached. Remove chops and tent with foil.

In the same skillet used for the chops, sear the tenderloin in remaining oil for 1 minute, turning often, until golden brown. Place in the oven and roast for 5–6 minutes, or until medium rare. Remove from oven, and tent with foil; allow to rest for 5 minutes before serving.

TO SERVE: In a saucepan, reheat the blanched turnips and carrots in boiling salted water for 1 minute; drain, return to saucepan, and toss in ½ remaining butter and olive oil. Follow the same procedure with the Savoy cabbage.

Cut each tenderloin into about 10 thin slices.

Divide the cabbage in 4 and pile high in the middle of 4 plates. Lean the venison chops on the cabbage. Place slices of tenderloin in a circle next to the chops. Arrange the carrots and turnips attractively on the plate, and spoon the Pinot Noir blueberry jus over and around the chops.

Darne of Georgian Bay Pike on a Bed of Fennel and Chanterelles

SERVES 4

2 onions, peeled
2 tbsp (30 mL) extra virgin
  olive oil
1 shallot, finely chopped
¼ cup (50 mL) white wine
¼ cup (50 mL) cold butter,
  cubed

1¼ tsp (6 mL) each, salt and
  pepper
2 tbsp (30 mL) lemon juice
4 darne of pike or pickerel fillets
1 fennel, sliced
¼ lb (125 g) chanterelles or other
  firm mushrooms, cleaned

(cut large mushrooms into
  quarters)
1 beefsteak tomato, seeded and
  diced
2 tbsp (30 mL) chives, finely
  chopped

Bring a pot of salted water to a boil and add the onions. Cook for 30–40 minutes, then drain and purée until smooth. Set aside.

In a deep skillet set over medium heat, heat 1 tbsp (15 mL) oil; add shallot and cook, stirring often, for 5 minutes, or until softened. Increase the heat to medium high, add the wine, and boil for 1 minute, or until reduced to 2 tbsp (30 mL).

Add the onion purée, and cook for 2 minutes, stirring often. Strain through a fine sieve into a clean saucepan. Slowly incorporate the butter by whisking in 1 cube at a time, until sauce is thickened. Season to taste with salt, pepper, and lemon juice. Keep warm.

In a steamer or a roasting pan fitted with a wire rack, bring 1 inch (2.5 cm) water to a boil. Season fish with salt and pepper. Place the fish on the steamer rack, and cover. Cook darne for 7–8

minutes, fillets for 5 minutes, or until fish is cooked through.

Blanch fennel in salted boiling water for approximately 3 minutes.

In a skillet over high heat, heat remaining oil; add chanterelles, and cook, stirring for 2 minutes, or until golden brown. Add the fennel and tomato; continue cooking for 1–2 minutes. Season to taste.

TO ASSEMBLE: On 4 warm plates, using the ragoût of fennel and chanterelles as a base, top with the darne of pike, pour the sauce all around. Sprinkle with the chopped chives.

Grouper à l'Alsacienne
with Braised Savoy Cabbage

SERVES 4

RECOMMENDED WINES:

Tokay
Clos Sainte Odile
Alsace

Pinot Gris
Bethel Heights Vineyard
Oreg0n

Chardonnay
Gaia e Rey
Angelo Gaja
Piedmont

SAUCE:

3 tbsp (45 mL) butter, cubed
½ cup (125 mL) finely chopped
   shallots
3 cups (750 mL) red wine
1½ cups (375 mL) port
1 cup (250 mL) fish stock (*p.100*)
2 cups (500 mL) veal stock
   (*p. 101*) or chicken stock
   (*p. 100*)
1 tbsp (15 mL) finely chopped
   tarragon

CABBAGE:

4 slices speck or bacon, chopped
1 onion, chopped
1 medium Savoy cabbage,
   shredded (about 10 cups/2.5 L)
½ tsp (2 mL) each, salt and
   pepper
½ cup (125 mL) Alsace Riesling
   or other dry white wine
¼ cup (50 mL) chicken stock
   (*p. 100*)
3 tbsp (45 mL) butter

1 tbsp (15 mL) chopped fresh
   chervil or parsley

GROUPER:

2 tbsp (30 mL) extra virgin
   olive oil
3 cloves garlic, halved
1 sprig each, rosemary and
   thyme
4 grouper fillets (about 8 oz/
   250 g each)
salt and pepper

TO PREPARE THE SAUCE: In a saucepan over medium-high heat, melt 1 tbsp (15 mL) butter; add shallots and cook until translucent, but not browned—about 5 minutes. Stir in wine and port; bring to a boil and simmer rapidly for 20 minutes or until reduced to about 1½ cups (375 mL). Add fish stock and veal stock, and continue simmering for 25 minutes, until reduced to 1½ cups (375 mL). Reduce heat to low; add remaining 2 tbsp (30 mL) butter, a little at a time, whisking constantly. Just before serving, add chopped tarragon.

TO PREPARE THE CABBAGE: In a large, deep sauté pan or wide saucepan over medium-high heat, cook speck/bacon until nicely browned—

about 5 minutes. Stir in onion, and cook, stirring often, for 5 minutes, or until softened. Add the cabbage, salt, and pepper. Pour in wine and chicken stock, cover pan and cook, stirring occasionally, until cabbage is tender. Stir in butter and chervil.

TO PREPARE THE GROUPER: In a large, oven-proof skillet, heat olive oil, garlic, and herbs over medium heat for 1–2 minutes. Pat grouper fillets dry, and season with salt and pepper; add to pan, and cook 3–4 minutes, turning once until browned on each side. Place pan uncovered in 400 F (200 C) oven for 4–5 minutes, or until fish is cooked but still slightly translucent in the centre.

TO SERVE: With a very sharp knife, thinly slice grouper fillets and fan on top of a mound of cabbage placed in the centre of each of 4 dinner plates. Drizzle sauce over the fillets.

Roasted Pears in Caramel Sauce

SERVES 4

4 cups (1 L) water
2½ cups (625 mL) granulated
   sugar
1 cup (250 mL) lemon juice
4 large bosc pears
1 tsp (5 mL) granulated sugar

CARAMEL SAUCE:
1 tsp (5 mL) butter
¾ cup (175 mL) granulated
   sugar
½ cup (125 mL) poaching liquid,
   from the pears
½ cup (125 mL) Poire William
   liqueur

GARNISH:
4 mint leaves
icing sugar to dust
Peel pears and reserve the skins
   for sauce.

TO PREPARE THE PEARS: Peel pears, and reserve skins for sauce. In a large pot set over medium-high heat, stir together water and sugar until sugar is dissolved. Bring to a boil, stir in lemon juice, and gently add pears.

Keep the pears submerged by placing a lid slightly smaller than the pot on top of the pears, or cut a circle of waxed paper to fit inside the pot on top of the pears, while they are poaching.

Simmer pears for 8–10 minutes or until easily pierced with a needle or toothpick. Remove pan from heat, and place uncovered on ice to cool.

When cooled, remove pears, reserving poaching liquid.

TO PREPARE THE CARAMEL SAUCE: In a medium-sized skillet over medium heat, melt the butter, stir in the reserved pear skins, and cook, stirring for 1 minute, or until fragrant. Stir in sugar; cook, stirring often, for about 5 minutes, or until beginning to turn brown. Add ½ cup (125 mL) of the poaching liquid, stir to combine, and simmer for 5–6 minutes, or until glossy and amber coloured. Remove from heat and immediately stir in Poire William liqueur. Strain through a fine mesh sieve. Set aside.

TO SERVE: Slice pears in half lengthwise, and remove the core with paring knife or grapefruit spoon. Place pear halves, cut side down, on a non-stick baking tray, and sprinkle with 1 tsp (5 mL) sugar. Place under broiler to caramelize, approximately 3 minutes, or until sugar is bubbly and golden brown.

Place 2 half-pears in the middle of each of 4 individual plates, ladle the sauce over and around each pear half. Dust the whole plate with icing sugar, and garnish with mint leaves.

RECOMMENDED WINES:

Château D'Yquem
Comte A. De-Lur Saluces
Sauternes

Ice Wine
Inniskillin
Ontario

Recioto I Capitelli
Az. Agr. Maculan
Veneto

Franco's Favourite Bread Pudding

SERVES 6 – 8

¼ cup (50 mL) cognac
½ cup (125 mL) raisins
1½ cups (375 mL) each, homo
   milk and 35% cream
1 vanilla bean, split lengthwise,
   or 1 tsp (5 ml) vanilla extract
5 eggs
2 egg yolks

1 cup (250 mL) granulated sugar
1 tsp (5 mL) butter
1 baguette, sliced thinly
¼ cup (50 mL) apricot jam
icing sugar

In a small saucepan, bring cognac and raisins to a simmer over medium-high heat; remove from heat, and let stand for 5 minutes.

Bring milk, cream, and vanilla bean to a boil over medium heat. In a large bowl, beat eggs and egg yolks until pale; gradually beat in the sugar. Continue beating for 2–3 minutes, or until pale and thick. Add the hot milk mixture, a little at a time, beating constantly.

Using the butter, grease a 10-inch (26-cm) round cake pan or other 8-cup (2-L) casserole. Arrange one layer of bread in a circle. Sprinkle with ¼ cup (50 mL) raisins. Top with remaining bread. Pour egg mixture over bread, being careful to soak each piece. Sprinkle with remaining raisins.

Place casserole dish in a roasting pan. Pour enough boiling water into the roasting pan to come 1 inch (2.5 cm) up side of dish. Put in 325 F

(160 C) oven for 45–55 minutes, or until a knife inserted in the middle of the pudding comes out clean.

Melt apricot jam in a small pan; brush over the pudding. Cool to room temperature. Just prior to serving, dust with icing sugar.

CHEF'S SUGGESTION: Sun-dried cherries, cranberries, or blueberries may be substituted for the raisins.

Warm Truffle–Centre Chocolate Ganache with Poire William Coulis

SERVES 4

RECOMMENDED WINES:

Tokaji Aszu Eszencia
Château Megyer
Hungary

Acini Nobili
Az. Agr. Maculan
Veneto

Late Harvest
Johannisburg Riesling
Robert Mondavi
Napa Valley

TRUFFLES:

2 oz (50 g) bittersweet chocolate

2 tbsp (30 mL) 35% cream

POIRE WILLIAM COULIS:

½ cup (125 mL) each, white wine and stock syrup *(p. 104)*

2 ripe pears, peeled, seeded, and chopped

½ stick of cinnamon

¼ cup (50 mL) Poire William liqueur

GANACHE:

4½ oz (125 g) bittersweet chocolate, chopped

2 tbsp (30 mL) butter, cubed

2 eggs

2 tbsp (30 mL) sugar

TO PREPARE THE TRUFFLES: Can be made up to a week in advance. Prepare at least one day prior to serving. Chop the chocolate into small pieces, and place in a mixing bowl.

In a saucepan, bring the cream to a simmer. Pour the cream over the chopped chocolate and let stand 1 minute. Stir until mixture takes on a smooth consistency.

Cover and refrigerate for about 4 hours. When the mixture is cold, use a teaspoon to roll into 4 balls, the size of truffles. Reserve in the refrigerator.

TO PREPARE THE POIRE WILLIAM COULIS: Bring all ingredients except the liqueur to a simmer in a saucepan, and cook for 10 minutes, or until the pears are soft enough to be mashed.

Remove and discard the cinnamon stick, and transfer mixture to a blender. Purée to a smooth consistency. Add the Poire William. Pass through a strainer, and reserve.

TO PREPARE THE GANACHE: Butter 4½-cup (125-mL) oven-proof ramekins or custard cups and line with parchment. In the top of a double boiler, melt the chocolate with the butter over simmering water. Remove from heat, and cool, stirring occasionally for 5 minutes, or until just barely warm.

Using an electric mixer, beat eggs until foamy; gradually add sugar. Continue beating for 2–3 minutes, or until thick enough to almost hold shape.

Pour ¼ of the egg mixture into the cooled chocolate; gently fold together until combined. Pour remaining egg mixture over chocolate and gently stir until combined but still streaky. Gently pour in enough batter to fill ramekins ¾ full. Place a truffle in the centre of each, and top with remaining batter. Place in 450 F (225 C) oven for 15–20 minutes.

TO SERVE: Pour warm Poire William coulis in the centre of each of 4 plates. Very gently tap bottom edge of ramekin on counter to loosen; tip out onto plate in centre of the coulis. Dust with icing sugar.

Winter

CHEF'S MENU

RECOMMENDED WINES:

*Meursault
Chartron et Trebuchet
Burgundy*

*Chardonnay
Long Vineyard
Napa Valley*

*Chardonnay
Montague Vineyard
Inniskillin
Ontario*

Croustillants Mille-Feuilles of Foie Gras and Salmon in Apple Emulsion

SERVES 4

2 Yukon Gold potatoes, peeled, dried, and very thinly sliced
⅓ cup (75 mL) butter, melted
¾ (3 mL) each, salt and pepper

1 tbsp (15 mL) lemon juice
½ cup (125 mL) apple juice
1 tbsp (15 mL) cold butter
1 lb (500 g) salmon fillet, skinned

½ lb (250 g) foie gras, sliced
2 tbsp (30 mL) vegetable oil
1 apple, julienned, to garnish

TO PREPARE THE POTATOES: Dip each potato slice in melted butter. In a cast-iron frying pan, cook the thinly sliced potatoes in remaining melted butter, over medium-high heat, until golden brown and crispy, about 4–5 minutes. Drain on paper towel, and sprinkle with salt and pepper.

TO PREPARE THE SAUCE: Bring the lemon juice and ¼ cup (50 mL) of the apple juice to a simmer in a small saucepan over medium heat for about 5 minutes, or until reduced to 2 tbsp (30 mL); add the remaining apple juice, and return to a boil.

Remove from heat, and place juice in a blender. Blend on high speed, adding the butter a little at a time to create a foamy emulsion.

TO PREPARE THE SALMON AND FOIE GRAS: Using a sharp 2½ -inch (6.5-cm) round cookie cutter, cut salmon into 8 circles and the foie gras into 4 circles. (Save scraps for another use.) Season each with remaining salt and pepper.

In a non-stick skillet over medium-high heat, heat 1 tbsp (15 mL) of the vegetable oil; add the salmon, and cook for 2 minutes per side, until medium rare.

Wipe pan clean, and reduce heat to medium; cook the foie gras in remaining oil for no more than 30–40 seconds per side, until golden brown.

TO ASSEMBLE: Create a mille-feuille on each of 4 dinner plates by layering a potato crisp, salmon tournedo, potato crisp, foie gras tournedo, potato crisp, salmon tournedo; top with potato crisp. Pour the apple emulsion around and over the mille-feuille, and garnish with julienne of apple.

Roasted Eggplant Soup

RECOMMENDED WINES:

*Gewürztraminer
(Eguisheim) Léon Beyer
Alsace*

*Sauvignon Blanc
Crystal Valley
Napa Valley*

*Salterio
Tenuta Trerose
Tuscany*

SERVES 6

2 large Italian eggplants, peeled and chopped
1 onion, chopped
½ cup (125 mL) carrot, chopped
¼ cup (50 mL) celery stalk, chopped
½ each, red and yellow pepper, chopped

1 clove garlic, peeled
¼ jalapeño pepper, chopped
2 tsp (10 mL) each, fresh oregano, basil, and rosemary
¼ cup (50 mL) extra virgin olive oil
1½ oz (45 g) prosciutto, wrapped in cheesecloth

4 cups (1 L) beef stock *(p.101)* or chicken stock *(p. 100)*
½ tsp (2 mL) each, salt and pepper
1 tbsp (15 mL) fresh lemon juice

In a large bowl, combine eggplant, onion, carrot, celery, peppers, garlic, jalapeño pepper, herbs, and olive oil (first 9 ingredients), stirring to coat evenly.

Spread out on baking sheet, and roast for 20–30 minutes in a hot oven, until golden brown. Transfer vegetables to a large pot with the prosciutto; add stock to cover. Season with salt and pepper. Bring to a boil; reduce heat to medium-low, and simmer for about 30 minutes, or until vegetables are very tender. Remove prosciutto from the stock, and discard. In batches, purée soup in food processor or blender. Return soup to pot, and adjust seasoning to taste, add lemon juice while reheating. Add more stock if necessary.

CHEF'S SUGGESTIONS: Garnish with sour cream, goat cheese, or purée of roasted red pepper. If cheesecloth is unavailable, use a coffee filter closed with a twist tie to wrap prosciutto.

Beef Carpaccio

S E R V E S 4

½ lb (250 g) beef tenderloin
½ cup (125 mL) extra virgin
   olive oil
3 tbsp (45 mL) lemon juice

1 tbsp (15 mL) each, chopped
   fresh chives and parsley
¼ tsp (1 mL) each, salt and
   pepper

1 lb (500 g) mushrooms
12 slices Parmigiano Reggiano
lollo rosso or other curly lettuce
black peppercorns, cracked

RECOMMENDED WINES:

*Rosso di Venegazzu Loredan
Gasparini
Veneto*

*Cabernet Franc
Az. Agr. Roberto Picech
Collio*

*Merlot
Villa Sandi
Veneto*

Place beef in freezer for 30 minutes. Meanwhile, in a small bowl, whisk together olive oil, lemon juice, chives, parsley, salt, and pepper. Reserve.

Using a very sharp knife, thinly slice beef tenderloin. With the side of knife, flatten each slice until paper thin.

TO ASSEMBLE: Clean the mushrooms, slice thinly, and arrange on the bottom of 4 individual chilled plates. Arrange Parmigiano slices over the mushrooms; lay the meat in a circular ring overlapping the cheese. Brush liberally with dressing. Place lollo rosso in the middle of the tenderloin, and drizzle the entire plate with dressing. Sprinkle liberally with cracked peppercorns. Garnish with additional Parmigiano slivers leaning on the lettuce.

CHEF'S SUGGESTIONS: Use fresh, never-frozen tenderloin. Prepared plates, undressed, can be covered and refrigerated for up to 1 hour before serving.

Tartare of Venison
with Black Truffle–Papaya Quenelles
and Chanterelle Salad

SERVES 4

RECOMMENDED WINES:

Shiraz
Presidents Select
Wolf Blass
Australia

Châteauneuf-du-Pape
Clos Saint Michel
Rhône

Brunello di Montaclino
Az. Agr. Lisini
Tuscany

MUSTARD OIL:

¼ cup (50 mL) mustard seeds, toasted

½ cup (125 mL) extra virgin olive oil

½ tsp (2 mL) turmeric

1 tsp (5 mL) dry mustard

2 tsp (10 mL) water

WALNUT VINAIGRETTE:

¼ cup (50 mL) balsamic vinegar

1 tbsp (15 mL) walnut oil

salt and pepper

TARTARE:

2 venison tenderloins (about 7 oz/200 g each), trimmed and finely chopped

½ tsp (2 mL) white truffle oil

¼ cup (50 mL) finely chopped shallots

pinch Chinese five-spice powder (p. 107)

½ tsp (2 mL) each, finely chopped fresh basil, rosemary, thyme, parsley, and chives

salt and pepper

PAPAYA QUENELLES:

1 papaya, peeled, seeded, and finely chopped

½ tsp (2 mL) white truffle oil

¼ cup (50 mL) finely chopped shallots

1 tbsp (15 mL) peeled, finely chopped, black truffle

1 tbsp (15 mL) lemon juice

CHANTERELLE SALAD:

1 tbsp (15 ml) extra virgin olive oil

¼ lb (125 g) chanterelle, porcini, or other mushrooms

½ tsp (2 mL) each, chopped fresh basil, rosemary, thyme, and parsley

¼ tsp (1 mL) each, salt and pepper

2 cups (500 mL) frisée, yellow part only

GARNISH:

4 curls Tête-de-Moine cheese, shaved in ruffles

1 plum tomato, seeded and finely chopped

sprigs of fresh chervil or parsley

TO PREPARE THE MUSTARD OIL: In a blender, combine toasted mustard seeds, olive oil, and turmeric. In a small cup, stir together dry mustard and water; add to blender. Purée on high until well combined. Transfer to a bowl, and cover and refrigerate. (Can be refrigerated for up to 5 days.)

Before serving, strain through a fine-mesh sieve.

TO PREPARE THE WALNUT VINAIGRETTE: In a measuring cup or bowl, whisk together balsamic vinegar and walnut oil. Stir in salt and pepper. Cover, and reserve.

TO PREPARE THE TARTARE: Gently mix together the venison, truffle oil, shallots, five-spice powder, chopped herbs, chives, salt, and pepper. Using a 2-inch (5-cm) round cookie cutter, shape venison into 12 equally thick patties. Transfer to a waxed paper-lined baking sheet; cover and refrigerate.

TO PREPARE THE PAPAYA QUENELLES: In a bowl, gently stir together papaya with truffle oil, chopped shallots, and black truffle. Just prior to serving, stir in the lemon juice. Using 2 teaspoons, form mixture into 12 egg-shaped quenelles. Reserve.

TO PREPARE THE CHANTERELLE SALAD: Sauté the mushrooms, basil, rosemary, thyme, parsley, salt, and pepper in the olive oil over high heat for 3–4 minutes, or until mushrooms are well browned. Cool to room temperature; toss with the frisée, and dress with walnut vinaigrette.

TO SERVE: Place equal portions of the chanterelle salad in the centre of each of 4 plates. Arrange 3 venison patties and 3 papaya quenelles around the edge of the plates. Drizzle the plates with mustard oil. Garnish with curls of Tête-de-Moine cheese, chopped tomato, and sprigs of chervil or parsley.

RECOMMENDED WINES:

Chardonnay
Az. Agr. Giovanni Bortoluzzi
Friuli

Terre di Tufo
Az. Agr. Teruzzi e Puthod
Tuscany

Clastidium
Az. Agr. Clastidio
Emilia Romagna

Fettuccine Natasha

SERVES 4

¾ lb (375 g) fettuccine
1 tbsp (15 mL) extra virgin
    olive oil
1 tbsp (15 mL) butter
1 garlic clove, minced
1 tbsp (15 mL) minced onion
4 medium tomatoes, seeded and
    diced

½ lb (250 g) smoked salmon,
    sliced
1 cup (250 mL) 35% cream
¼ cup (50 mL) vodka
¼ tsp (1 mL) pepper
1 oz (28 g) caviar (optional)

In a large pot of boiling salted water, cook fettuccine until *al dente*. Drain, and set aside.

In a large skillet, heat the olive oil and butter. Stir in garlic and onion, and sauté, stirring often, for 2 minutes, until fragrant. Add the tomatoes, and bring to a boil. Reduce heat and simmer for 5 minutes, or until softened and beginning to thicken.

Stir in the smoked salmon, cream, and vodka; simmer for 5 minutes, or until thick enough to coat the back of a spoon. Gently fold in cooked pasta and pepper. Garnish with a rosette of smoked salmon or caviar.

CHEF'S SUGGESTION: If a saltier taste is desired, add the smoked salmon at the same time as the tomatoes.

Quail with Leek Fondue and Fig, Balsamic Vinegar, and Ice Wine Jus

SERVES 4

LEEK FONDUE:
3 tbsp (45 mL) butter

1½ cups (375 mL) chopped leeks

2 tbsp (30 mL) Ice Wine

2 plum tomatoes, seeded and chopped

2 tbsp (30 mL) chopped chives

¼ tsp (1 mL) salt and pepper

ICE WINE JUS:
1 tsp (5 mL) extra virgin olive oil

½ cup (125 mL) chopped shallots

1 tbsp (15 mL) balsamic vinegar

1 cup (250 mL) Ice Wine

2 tbsp (30 mL) butter, cubed

8 fresh figs

1 tsp (5 mL) lemon juice

¼ tsp (1 mL) each, salt and pepper

1 tsp (5 mL) brown sugar

QUAIL:
2 tbsp (30 mL) extra virgin olive oil

4 jumbo quail, deboned and halved

½ tsp (2 mL) each, salt and pepper

TO PREPARE THE LEEK FONDUE: Melt butter in a skillet over medium heat; stir in leeks and cover. Cook for 5 minutes, stirring occasionally. Increase heat and cook 3–4 minutes to brown slightly; add Ice Wine, tomatoes, and chives. Season to taste with salt and pepper. Set aside.

TO PREPARE THE ICE WINE JUS: In a saucepan, heat olive oil over medium heat and stir in shallots. Cook for 5 minutes, or until translucent. Stir in balsamic vinegar and continue cooking for 1 minute. Increase heat to medium-high; pour in Ice Wine and cook for about 2 minutes, until reduced to ¾. Whisk in the butter, bit by bit, until sauce is thickened. Cut 4 of the figs into quarters lengthwise. Mix them into the sauce with lemon juice, salt, and pepper; reserve.

Cut the remaining 4 figs almost through to the base, into 6 wedges. Squeeze base of the fig gently so that wedges fan out to resemble tulip petals. Place on a rimmed baking sheet; sprinkle exposed flesh with brown sugar. Set aside.

TO PREPARE THE QUAIL: Heat olive oil in a clean skillet over medium-high heat; add quail, meaty side down and cook for 3–4 minutes, until well browned, turning once. Transfer quail to the baking sheet with the figs and place in a 500 F (260 C) oven for 2–3 minutes, or until quail are medium rare and figs are well caramelized. Season with salt and pepper.

TO SERVE: Place quail on a bed of leek fondue on 4 individual plates, and drizzle with the jus. Garnish plates with the fig tulips and chives.

Polenta with Mascarpone and Fresh Black Truffles

RECOMMENDED WINES:

Barolo
La Serra
Az. Agr. Poderi Marcarini
Piedmont

Amarone della Valpolicella
Mazzano
Az Agr. Masi
Veneto

Valpolicella Classico
Az. Agr. Guiseppe Quintarelli
Veneto

SERVES 4

⅓ cup (75 mL) mascarpone cheese

6 cups (1.5 L) chicken stock (p. 100)

½ lb (250 g) fine cornmeal

2 tsp (10 mL) butter

salt and pepper

1 small black truffle

Lightly butter 4 dinner plates. Make a mound in the centre of each with equal amounts of mascarpone cheese. Refrigerate the plates until needed.

In a large saucepan, heat stock until boiling. Reduce heat to medium; in a slow, steady stream, stirring constantly, pour in cornmeal. Stir until thickened, about 3 minutes. Reduce heat to low and cook, stirring often, for 30 minutes, or until polenta is creamy and very thick. Season cooked polenta with salt and pepper.

TO SERVE: Spoon over cold mascarpone on the prepared plates, covering the cheese completely. Slice the truffle over the polenta while warm, and serve immediately.

CHEF'S SUGGESTION: Instant polenta cornmeal may be substituted to reduce the cooking time by half.

Tian of West Coast Scallops
in Pastel Saffron Sauce

SERVES 4

RECOMMENDED WINES:

Pinot Grigio
Cabert
Friuli

Chardonnay
Robert Mondavi
Napa Valley

Meursault
J.M. Boillot
Burgundy

SAUCE:

1 tbsp (15 mL) butter
1 cup (250 mL) finely chopped
  shallots
¼ cup (50 mL) Riesling
¼ cup (50 mL) fish stock *(p. 100)*
¼ cup (50 mL) 35% cream
1 tbsp (15 mL) lemon juice
pinch saffron
¼ tsp (1 mL) each, salt and
  pepper

RATATOUILLE:

1 tbsp (15 mL) each, extra virgin
  olive oil and butter
1 small red onion, chopped
pinch chopped fresh thyme
1 each, small yellow and green
  zucchini, chopped
1 each, yellow and red pepper,
  finely chopped
2 plum tomatoes, seeded and
  chopped
½ tsp (2 mL) each, salt and
  pepper

SPINACH:

1 tsp (5 mL) butter
8 cups (2 L) spinach leaves
¼ tsp (1 mL) each, salt and
  pepper

SCALLOPS:

8 sea scallops
1 tbsp (15 mL) extra virgin
  olive oil
pinch each, salt and pepper
chervil and parsley

TO PREPARE THE SAUCE: Sauté chopped shallots in 1 tbsp (15 mL) butter over medium-high heat, stirring often until softened—about 5 minutes. Stir in wine; increase heat to high and boil for 3 minutes, until reduced to 2 tbsp (30 mL). Add fish stock, and continue to cook for another 3 minutes, or until reduced to ¼ cup (50 mL). Remove from heat; stir in cream, lemon juice, and saffron. Allow to rest for 5 minutes; season to taste with salt and pepper. Pass through a fine sieve into a clean pot, and set aside.

TO PREPARE THE RATATOUILLE: In a large deep skillet, melt butter and oil together over medium heat; stir in onion and thyme, and cook for 5 minutes until softened. Increase heat to medium high, add zucchini and peppers, and cook for another 5 minutes until browned. Stir in chopped tomatoes, season to taste with salt and pepper; cook for 1 minute. Reserve.

TO PREPARE THE SPINACH: In a deep skillet set over high heat, melt the butter and add the spinach; cover and cook for 45 seconds, until just wilted and bright green. Season with salt and pepper. Drain in colander.

TO PREPARE THE SCALLOPS: Trace 4 3½-inch (8.75-cm) circles on parchment paper using a cookie cutter or tart ring. Slice the scallops ¼ inch

(8 mm) thick, and place them on and around the paper in a circular fashion, overlapping the slices. Drizzle with a little olive oil, and season with salt and pepper. Place in 400 F (200 C) oven for about 5 minutes, until opaque but not dry and rubbery.

TO ASSEMBLE: Place a 4-inch (10-cm) tart ring or circular cookie cutter in the middle of a hot plate; spoon ratatouille of vegetables into the centre to fill it halfway; gently pack down with the back of a spoon. Place drained spinach on top in an even layer. Remove the cookie cutter. Using a metal spatula, gently lift the sea scallops off the paper onto the tower of spinach. Pour the saffron sauce on top and around the tian, and garnish with bouquet of chervil and parsley.

Swordfish with Two Sauces

SERVES 4

4 swordfish steaks (5 oz/150 g
   each)

MARINADE:

1 tbsp (15 mL) extra virgin olive
   oil

1 tbsp (15 mL) chopped fresh
   rosemary

2 cloves garlic, minced

BUTTER SAUCE:

½ cup (125 mL) butter, chilled
   and cubed

¼ cup (50 mL) chopped shallots

¼ cup (50 mL) white wine

1 cup (250 mL) fish stock *(p. 100)*

¼ cup (50 mL) lemon juice

pinch each, salt, pepper, and
   cayenne

RED WINE SAUCE:

½ cup (125 mL) port

¼ cup (50 mL) each, heavy red
   wine (Barolo) and balsamic
   vinegar

GARNISH:

1 tbsp (15 mL) each, chives and
   parsley, chopped

RECOMMENDED WINES:

Chardonnay
Far Niente
Napa Valley

Puligny-Montrachet
Clos de la Garenne
L. Jadot
Burgundy

Il Marzocco
Az. Agr. Avignonesi
Tuscany

TO PREPARE THE MARINADE: In a shallow dish, combine olive oil, rosemary, and garlic. Add fish, turning to coat; cover and refrigerate 1 hour.

TO PREPARE THE BUTTER SAUCE: In a saucepan over medium heat, melt 1 tbsp (15 mL) of the butter. Add the shallots, stirring often for 5 minutes. Add white wine, fish stock, and lemon juice; bring to a boil, reduce heat, and simmer for 10–12 minutes, or until reduced to about ½ cup (125 mL). Whisking constantly, add remaining butter bit by bit. Season with salt, pepper, and cayenne. Strain and keep warm.

TO PREPARE THE RED WINE SAUCE: In small saucepan, combine port, red wine, and balsamic vinegar; bring to a boil. Reduce heat, and simmer about 20 minutes, or until reduced to about 2 tbsp (30 mL). Stir in 2 tbsp (30 mL) butter sauce.

TO PREPARE THE FISH: Remove fish from marinade. In a large skillet on medium-high heat, warm fish marinade to a simmer. Add fish, and cook, turning once, for 8–10 minutes, or until golden brown.

TO ASSEMBLE: Pour butter sauce around edge of plate, splash with red wine sauce. Using a knife, draw sauces into each other to make a web-like pattern; place the swordfish in centre. Garnish with chopped chives and parsley.

RECOMMENDED WINES:

*Chardonnay
Reserve
E. & J. Gallo
Sonoma*

*Chassagne Montrachet
1er Cru
M. Chenu
Burgundy*

*Chardonnay
Franco Benincasa
Friuli*

Roasted Red Snapper
with Citrus Nage

SERVES 4

CITRUS NAGE:

⅔ cup (150 mL) jus de nage
  (p. 104)
8 segments pink grapefruit,
  chopped
1 tbsp (15 mL) extra virgin
  olive oil
2 tbsp (30 mL) butter
¼ tsp (1 mL) each, salt and white
  pepper
12 leaves coriander, finely
  chopped
1 tsp (5 mL) green peppercorns

FISH:

4½ oz (150 g) red snapper fillets
flour to dust
salt and pepper to taste
1 tbsp (15 mL) extra virgin
  olive oil
sprig each, rosemary and thyme
12 segments each, orange and
  grapefruit

CANDIED CITRUS PEEL AND
  GINGER ROOT:

12 each, lemon, lime, and
  grapefruit zest, julienned
12 paper thin slices of fresh
  ginger root, peeled and finely
  julienned
1 cup stock syrup *(p. 104)*
1 tbsp (15 mL) champagne
  vinegar

TO PREPARE THE CITRUS NAGE: Bring the jus de nage to a boil in a saucepan. Add the grapefruit segments; cook, stirring occasionally, for about 5 minutes, or until grapefruit is breaking down. Transfer to blender and purée until smooth; incorporate olive oil, butter, salt, and pepper; blend until frothy. Add chopped coriander and green peppercorns. Keep warm.

TO PREPARE THE FISH: Dust fish fillets with a mixture of flour, salt, and pepper.

Over medium-high heat, in a large skillet, heat oil; add fish fillets, skin side down, and cook for 3–4 minutes, turning once until browned. Add sprigs of rosemary and thyme. Set aside.

TO PREPARE THE CANDIED PEEL AND GINGER: Place zest and ginger in colander, and scald with boiling water; refresh with cold water immediately. In a small saucepan, cover the julienne of zest and ginger with 1 cup (250 mL) of stock syrup and bring to a boil; poach for about 15 minutes. Remove from the heat; stir in champagne vinegar, and leave to cool.

Put orange and grapefruit segments in an oven-proof plate with fish fillets. Place in 400 F (200 C) oven for 5 minutes, or until fish is cooked and fruit is heated through.

TO SERVE: Place the fish fillets in the centre of each of 4 dinner plates, surround with grapefruit and orange segments, and drizzle with citrus nage. Sprinkle the plate with candied zest and ginger root.

Centro Veal Chop

SERVES 4

RECOMMENDED WINES:

*Venagazzu
Black Label
Venagazzu Vini
Veneto*

*Barbarossa
Fattoria Paradiso
Emilia Romagna*

*Sassicaia
Marchesi Incisa della Rocchetta
Tuscany*

VEGETABLES
1 tbsp (15 mL) butter
6 peeled whole garlic cloves
½ cup (125 mL) pearl onions, peeled
3 carrots, cut on the diagonal
4 new potatoes, thinly sliced
¾ cup (175 mL) snow peas, stems removed
4 green onions, cut into 1 inch (2.3 cm) pieces
½ tsp (2 mL) each, salt and pepper
¾ cup (175 mL) veal stock (p.101) or chicken stock (p. 100)
2 tbsp (30 mL) freshly grated Parmesan cheese

VEAL CHOP
1 tbsp (15 mL) each, butter and extra virgin olive oil
2 whole garlic cloves, sliced
4 centre-cut veal chops (9–10 oz/275 g each)
½ cup (125 mL) white wine
1 cup (250 mL) veal stock (p. 101) or chicken stock (p. 100)
1 tsp (5 mL) truffle oil (optional)

TO PREPARE VEGETABLES: In a large cast-iron frying pan, melt 1 tbsp (15 mL) butter over medium-high heat. Add garlic, onions, carrots, and potato slices. Cook, turning often, for 5–7 minutes, or until golden brown. In boiling salted water, cook the snow peas and green onions for 1 minute, until bright green; drain, and immediately immerse in cold water. Drain well, and stir into browned vegetables. Season with salt and pepper. Pour in enough veal stock to just cover the vegetables. Place in a 350 F (180 C) oven for 20 minutes, or until potatoes and carrots are tender and the stock has been absorbed. Sprinkle with Parmesan cheese, and broil for 1 minute. Set aside, covered with foil, to keep warm.

TO PREPARE VEAL CHOP: In a large frying pan, warm olive oil and butter over medium-high heat. Add garlic slices, and cook 1 minute, until

fragrant. Add veal chops, and cook for 15–17 minutes, turning once. Remove veal chops from the pan, and place on a warm platter; tent with foil.

Using the same pan, bring white wine to a boil, stirring to incorporate remaining veal bits. Cook for 3 minutes, or until reduced to 2 tbsp (30 mL). Add veal stock, and simmer 5 minutes, or until thickened and reduced enough to coat the back of a spoon. Whisk in truffle oil; strain and reserve.

TO SERVE: Remove whole garlic cloves, and arrange vegetables in an attractive manner in the middle of 4 individual plates. Lean the veal chop on the vegetables and pour the jus around the meat. Top each chop with a clove of the braised garlic.

Pinot Noir
"Resérve Personelle"
Hugel
Alsace

Rosso di Montalcino
La chiesa di San Restituta
Tuscany

Braccano
Az. Agr. Enzo Mecella
Marche

Braised Tripe and Langoustines with Leek and Vegetable Fondue

SERVES 4

1 lb (500 g) tripe
½ cup (125 mL) butter
½ cup (125 mL) each finely chopped leeks, carrots, and onions
¼ tsp (1 mL) Chinese five-spice powder *(p. 107)*
2 whole cloves
2 cloves garlic, minced

⅓ cup (75 mL) dry apple cider
⅓ cup (75 mL) Calvados
½ cup (125 mL) chanterelles
½ tsp (2 mL) each, salt and pepper
1½ cup (375 mL) beet greens, chopped in 1-inch (2.5-cm) strips
¼ cup (50 mL) lobster jus *(p. 102)*

6 each, blanched baby beets, carrots, and turnip
1 cup (250 mL) blanched, julienned leeks
16 cooked, peeled langoustines or 16 tiger shrimp, peeled and cooked
1 tbsp (15 mL) chopped chives

Italians treat tripe with as much respect as we do the hot dog; it is as readily available on the streets of Florence as are hot dogs on Toronto street corners.

Cut tripe in strips about ½ inch (1 cm) wide. In ovenproof pot over low heat, melt 7 tbsp (100 mL) butter; stir in tripe, leeks, carrots, onions, five-spice powder, cloves, and garlic. Cover tripe and vegetables with cider and Calvados. Cover pot, and braise in 275 F (140 C) oven for 4½–5 hours, or until tripe is very soft.

Remove from oven, drain off liquid and vegetables, reserving ½ cup (125 mL) of braising liquid.

In a skillet set over medium heat, melt remaining butter and sauté the chanterelles. Season to taste with salt and pepper; add beet greens, and cook

for 1 minute, until wilted but still green. Reserve. In a large saucepan over medium heat, place reserved braising liquid; add tripe, and heat through; stir in lobster jus and blanched vegetables, chanterelles, beet greens, and langoustines. Stir carefully for 1 minute to heat through. Season to taste.

CHEF'S SUGGESTION: Serve, at table, on an Italian country-style platter with garnish of chopped chives.

Ice Wine Semifreddo in Buckwheat Cups

SERVES 4

SEMIFREDDO:

⅔ cup (175 mL) 35% cream

2 eggs, separated

1 tbsp (15 mL) liquid honey

⅓ cup (75 mL) Ice Wine, at room
   temperature

2 tbsp (30 mL) granulated sugar

BUCKWHEAT CUPS:

1 egg white, beaten

⅓ cup (75 mL) icing sugar, sifted

2 tbsp (30 mL) melted butter

¼ tsp (1 mL) vanilla

¼ cup (50 mL) buckwheat flour

2½ tbsp (40 mL) ground almonds

pinch salt

TO PREPARE THE SEMIFREDDO: Using a hand mixer, whip cream until thick and light—about 1–2 minutes. Clean beaters, and beat egg yolks on high speed, until thick and pale yellow. Beat in honey and Ice Wine.

In a clean, dry bowl, beat the two egg whites until frothy. Gradually add sugar, and continue beating for about 2 minutes, until mixture forms soft peaks.

Using a rubber spatula, gently fold whipped cream into yolk mixture. Fold egg whites into mixture until just combined; spoon into lightly greased muffin tin or 4 tea cups. Cover, and freeze for 4 hours, or overnight.

TO PREPARE THE BUCKWHEAT CUPS: In a small bowl, whisk together egg white, icing sugar, butter, and vanilla. Stir in flour, almonds, and salt.

On a chilled, greased baking sheet, spread batter very thinly, with the back of a spoon, into 3-inch (7-cm) circles. Bake in a 325 F (160 C) oven for 7–8 minutes, or until edges are beginning to brown. Immediately remove from pan, and place over inverted teacups. Gently press edges to mould shape of cups. Allow to cool completely.

TO SERVE: Remove semifreddo from cups by quickly dipping bottoms into hot water. Turn out into buckwheat cups.

RECOMMENDED WINES:

Late Harvest Riesling
Inniskillin
Ontario

Cuvée d'Or
Kalin Cellars
Marin County

Moscato Passito di Pantelleria
Az. Agr. Vecchio Samperi
Sicily

CHEF'S SUGGESTION:
Serve with fresh seasonal fruits or berries.

Jasmine Rice Pudding with Dried Fruit in Warm Spy Apple Soup

SERVES 6

RECOMMENDED WINES:

Dolce
Far Niente
Napa Valley

Verduzzo di Ramandolo
Az. Agr. Giovanni Dri
Friuli

Vin Santo
Castello di Querceto
Tuscany

PUDDING:

½ cup (125 mL) Jasmine or
    fragrant Thai rice
1¼ cup (300 mL) milk
1 cup (250 mL) water
1 egg
¼ cup (50 mL) granulated sugar
⅓ cup (75 mL) 35% cream
1 tbsp (15 mL) finely chopped
    pickled ginger

DRIED FRUIT:

½ cup (125 mL) dried apricots,
    sliced
⅓ cup (75 mL) each, blueberries
    and dried sour cherries
1 tbsp (15 mL) each, Grand
    Marnier and cognac
½ cup (125 mL) water

APPLE SOUP:

1⅓ cups (325 mL) water
¾ cup (175 mL) apple cider
¼ cup (50 mL) sugar
¼ cup (50 mL) lemon juice
½ vanilla bean
2 large Spy apples, peeled, cored,
    and diced
pinch of cinnamon
6 mint leaves

TO PREPARE THE PUDDING: Rinse rice under running cold water. In a saucepan over high heat, combine rice with 1 cup (250 mL) milk and the water. Bring to a boil; reduce heat, and simmer until liquid is evaporated and rice is cooked.

Whisk egg with sugar; add cream, the remaining ¼ cup (50 mL) milk, and the chopped ginger; stir in the cooked rice. Lightly grease 6 ramekins with a bit of butter, and spoon in the rice pudding. Place ramekins in a pan of boiling water (bain marie) in 300 F (150 C) oven for 25–30 minutes.

TO PREPARE THE FRUIT: In a saucepan set over medium-high heat, boil the apricots, blueberries, and sour cherries in Grand Marnier, cognac, and water for 2–3 minutes. Drain and set aside.

TO PREPARE THE APPLE SOUP: Over medium-high heat, bring to the boil water, cider, sugar, and lemon juice; add the vanilla, apples, and cinnamon; reduce heat, and simmer until liquid is reduced by ⅓. Remove from heat, remove vanilla bean, and purée apples in a food processor or blender until smooth.

TO SERVE: On 6 individual warm large pasta plates, arrange the dried fruit. Turn out pudding into centre of fruit, and pour apple soup around the rice. Garnish with mint leaves.

Spring

CHEF'S MENU

Salad of Artichokes,
Sea Scallops, and Crab,
with Caviar Vinaigrette
page 80

Feuilletés of Morels, White
Asparagus, and Escargot,
in Ice Wine Emulsion
page 81

Le Trou Normand
page 99

Ontario Spring Lamb
Tenderloin with Herb
and Citrus Jus
page 94

Fresh Berry Napoleon
with Lemon Curd
page 98

RECOMMENDED WINES:

Riesling Wolfberger
Alsace

Chardonnay
Elk Cove Vineyards
Oregon

Chardonnay
Az. Agr. La Spinona
Piedmont

Salad of Artichokes, Sea Scallops, and Crab, with Caviar Vinaigrette

SERVES 4

VINAIGRETTE:

2 tbsp (30 mL) red wine vinegar
salt and pepper
½ cup (125 mL) extra virgin
  olive oil
1 tbsp (15 mL) caviar
1 tbsp (15 mL) chopped fresh
  chives

CRAB:

4 oz (125 g) cooked Dungeness
  crab
2 tsp (10 mL) extra virgin
  olive oil
2 tsp (10 mL) chopped fresh
  chives
1 tsp (5 mL) chopped fresh
  tarragon
½ tsp (2 mL) lemon juice
salt and pepper

SCALLOPS:

12 sea scallops
2 tbsp (30 mL) each, chopped
  fresh chervil and parsley
salt and pepper
1 tbsp (15 mL) butter
4 artichoke hearts, cooked and
  quartered
1 tbsp (15 mL) lemon juice
4 cups (1 L) mesclun greens

TO PREPARE THE VINAIGRETTE: Place red wine vinegar in a bowl. Add a pinch of salt and pepper, and stir to dissolve. Whisk in the olive oil, until mixture forms an emulsion. This will keep in the refrigerator for up to a week. Just before serving, add the caviar and finely chopped chives.

TO PREPARE THE CRAB: Shred crab into bite-sized pieces. In a bowl, toss crab meat together with olive oil, chives, tarragon, lemon juice, salt, and pepper. Cover, and refrigerate until ready to use.

TO PREPARE THE SCALLOPS: Toss sea scallops with chervil and salt and pepper to season. Melt butter in a non-stick skillet; add the scallops, and sear over medium-high heat for 2–3 minutes, until browned. Add the artichoke hearts and lemon juice, stirring to coat in pan juices.

TO SERVE: Arrange mesclun greens in the middle of 4 individual plates. Place 3 sea scallops around the lettuce, and top with equal amounts of crab meat. Carefully place sliced artichoke hearts around the perimeter of the plates, and drizzle with the caviar vinaigrette.

Feuilletés of Morels, White Asparagus, and Escargot, in Ice Wine Emulsion

SERVES 4

½ lb (250 g) puff pastry

1 egg, beaten

¼ cup (50 mL) butter, cubed

½ cup (125 mL) finely chopped shallots

½ cup (125 mL) morels, halved and dried

24 escargot

½ cup (125 mL) Ice Wine

¼ cup (50 mL) apple juice

¼ tsp (15 mL) each, salt and pepper

16 white asparagus tips, blanched

1 tbsp (15mL) chives, chopped

RECOMMENDED WINES:

Pinot Blanc
Au Bon Climat
Santa Barbara

Pouilly Fuissé
Louis Jadot
Burgundy

Soave Classico
Az. Agr. Roberto Anselmi
Veneto

On a cold, lightly floured counter top, roll out the puff pastry into a 4 x 8 inch (10 x 20 cm) rectangle. Cut into 4 smaller rectangles, 4 x 2 inch (10 x 5 cm) each. Refrigerate for 1 hour covered. Transfer to baking sheet; brush tops lightly with beaten egg; and bake in 400 F (200 C) oven for 10 minutes, until golden brown and heated through.

In a skillet set over medium-high heat, melt 1 tbsp (15 mL) butter; add half the shallots, and cook, stirring, for 1 minute. Add morels, and cook until lightly browned. Remove to heated platter.

In the same pan, melt 1 tbsp (15 mL) of butter; add the remaining shallots. Sauté for 1 minute; add the escargot and cook for another minute, until heated through. Add the Ice Wine and apple juice, and boil to reduce slightly. Drain through a sieve into a clean pan; add shallots and escargot to platter with the morels.

Bring liquid to a boil, and whisk in remaining butter cubes; add salt and pepper to taste. Add morel mixture, and asparagus, to the sauce. Gently heat through.

TO ASSEMBLE: With a sharp knife, divide the puff-pastry rectangles in half vertically. Set bottom half in the centre of each of 4 individual plates. Top with equal amounts of morel–escargot–asparagus mixture. Set the pastry tops leaning against the feuilleté; drizzle remaining sauce around the plate. Garnish with chopped chives.

RECOMMENDED WINES:

Fume Blanc
Chateau St. Jean
Sonoma

Pinot Blanc
Cuvée Les Amours Hugel
Alsace

Vernaccia Riserva
Gucciardini Strozzi
Tuscany

Soupe de Légumes au Pistou

SERVES 4

SOUPE:

3 oz (80 g) bacon, chopped

1 small onion, chopped

½ cup (125 mL) each, chopped celery, leeks, carrots, and turnip

6 cups (1.5 L) chicken stock (p. 100)

1 cup peeled and diced potato

1 plum tomato, peeled, seeded, and diced

½ cup (125 mL) green beans, cut in 1 inch (2.5 cm) lengths

½ cup (125 mL) cooked fava beans

½ cup (125 mL) zucchini, diced

4 oz (100 g) sea scallops, about 8 scallops

PISTOU:

3 cloves garlic, peeled

1 cup (250 mL) basil leaves, loosely packed

¼ cup (50 mL) freshly grated Parmesan cheese

¼ cup (50 mL) extra virgin olive oil

salt and pepper

TO PREPARE THE SOUP: In a soup pot over medium heat, cook bacon for 2 minutes, or until brown; stir in onion, celery, leeks, carrots, and turnip. Cook, stirring often for 5 minutes, or until translucent. Pour in chicken stock, and bring to a boil. Reduce heat to medium-low and simmer for 30 minutes. Add potato, and simmer for 15 minutes. Add the tomato, green beans, fava beans, and zucchini. Simmer for another 10 minutes. Reserve.

TO PREPARE THE PISTOU: In a blender, purée the garlic, basil, and Parmesan cheese until smooth; with motor running, slowly drizzle in the oil. Season with salt and pepper.

TO SERVE: Cut scallops in ½, and place in hot soup plates; put a dollop of pistou in each bowl, and ladle in hot soup. Serve immediately.

CHEF'S SUGGESTION: The hot soup served in the hot bowl will cook the scallops to tender. The remaining pistou may be served as additional condiment.

Atlantic Salmon Tataki
with Sesame Cucumber Noodles

SERVES 4

1 cucumber, peeled and seeded
1¼ tsp (6 mL) salt
1 lb (500 g) Atlantic salmon,
   centre-cut fillet, skinned
3 tbsp (45 mL) sesame oil
½ tsp (2 mL) granulated sugar
¼ tsp (1 mL) pepper

¼ cup (50 mL) lime juice
1 tsp (5 mL) finely grated lime
   zest
2 tbsp (30 mL) light soy sauce
1 tbsp (15 mL) sesame seeds,
   roasted

1 green onion, sliced, on an angle
coriander leaves
1 red chili pepper, cleaned,
   seeded, and diced

RECOMMENDED WINES:

Prosecco
Primo Franco
Veneto

Iron Horse
Sparkling Brut
Sonoma

Veuve Clicquot
Brut-Champagne

Slice cucumber lengthwise. Using a coarse grater, shred the cucumber into long, thin, noodle-width strips. Place in a colander, and sprinkle with 1 tsp (5 mL) salt. Let drain for about 30 minutes.

Rub salmon with 1 tsp (5 mL) sesame oil, sugar, ¼ tsp (1 mL) salt, and ¼ tsp (1 mL) pepper. Leave for 1 hour, then rinse under cold running water, pat dry with a paper towel.

Sear all sides of the salmon, either over a direct flame or in a heavy non-stick pan or griddle. Mix together the lime juice, zest, soy sauce, sesame seeds, and remaining oil, and toss with the cucumber. Season to taste with salt and pepper. Take a fork and twist the cucumber spaghetti around the tines and arrange a mound on each of 4 dinner plates. Top with thin slices of salmon.

Sprinkle entirely with the green onion, a few coriander leaves, and the red chili pepper.

Spinach-Ricotta Gnocchi

S E R V E S   6

10 oz (300 g) spinach, cleaned
    and stems removed
2 eggs, beaten
1 tub ricotta cheese (474 g)

2¾ cups (675 mL) all-purpose
    flour
¼ tsp (1 mL) each, salt, pepper,
    and nutmeg

RECOMMENDED WINES:

Chardonnay
Mayacamus
Napa Valley

Condrieu
E. Guigal
Rhône

Vite Bianca
Ornella Molon
Veneto

In a large pot, over medium heat, cook spinach for 1 minute until wilted. Cool under running water; squeeze excess moisture from spinach; purée in food processor or blender. Add eggs and ricotta; process until smooth.

In a large bowl, combine flour, salt, pepper, and nutmeg. Make a well in the centre of the flour mixture, and pour in the spinach mixture. Stir to form a sticky dough.

Transfer mixture to a piping bag without a tip.

Pipe long rows of batter onto waxed paper–lined baking sheets. Cover, and refrigerate for 30 minutes, or until chilled through.

Using a greased knife, cut dough into 1¼-inch (3-cm) long pieces to form gnocchi.

In a large pot of boiling salty water, cook gnocchi for 1½–2 minutes, or until they float. Drain well.

CHEF'S SUGGESTION: Makes an excellent accompaniment for grilled fish.

RECOMMENDED WINES:

Ribolla Gialla
Az. Agr. Angoris
Friuli

Sauvignon Blanc
Lois Honig
Napa Valley

Riesling Italico
Az. Agr. Francesco Gravner
Friuli

Asparagus with Mousseline Sauce

SERVES 6

2 lb (1 kg) large white asparagus
1 cup (250 mL) butter
4 egg yolks
2 tbsp (30 mL) champagne
   vinegar

1 tbsp (15 mL) water
pinch each, salt, white pepper,
   and cayenne
2 tbsp (30 mL) 35% cream

Snap off woody ends of asparagus at natural breaking point. In wide skillet or large deep pot, cook asparagus for 10–12 minutes in salted water, until tender. White asparagus should not be served crisp, but the green asparagus may be.

In a small saucepan or ovenproof dish, melt butter. Using a spoon, skim froth from surface and discard. Allow butter to cool slightly.

In another saucepan, whisk together egg yolks, champagne vinegar, water, salt, pepper, and cayenne. Whisk for 30 seconds, or until thoroughly combined and pale yellow. Place the saucepan over water in a double boiler; whisk continuously for 2–3 minutes, or until the mixture draws ribbons and is doubled in volume. Pour in the butter, a little at a time, whisking until completely blended. Keep warm. Just before serving, add the cream, adjust seasoning. Serve the mousseline sauce warm.

Calf's Liver alla Veneziana

SERVES 6

2 lb (1 kg) calf's liver
¼ cup (50 mL) butter
3 onions, thinly sliced
½ cup (125 mL) dry white wine
¼ cup (50 mL) veal stock (p. 101)

salt and freshly ground pepper, to
 taste
2 tbsp (30 mL) finely chopped
 parsley

RECOMMENDED WINES:

Realda
Az. Agr. Roberto Anselmi
Veneto

Rosso
Villa Sandi
Veneto

Merlot del Piave
Az. Agr. Mazzolada
Veneto

Peel off the translucent membrane covering the liver. Slice the liver into very thin, medium-sized strips.

Melt 2 tbsp (30 mL) of butter in a skillet over medium heat; add onions and cook, stirring occasionally, for 5 minutes, or until softened. Increase the heat to medium high, and continue cooking until golden brown. Add the wine, stock, salt, and pepper; braise, stirring often, for 10 minutes. Remove the onions from pan, and keep warm.

Melt remaining butter over high heat; add the liver, and sauté for 1–2 minutes until just cooked through. Add salt and pepper to taste. Serve liver on bed of braised onions and sprinkle with chopped parsley.

CHEF'S SUGGESTION: Serve with soft or grilled polenta.

The success of this dish depends on the liver, which must be cooked over high heat very briefly so that it does not become tough and dry. The onions, therefore, should be cooked separately.

RECOMMENDED WINES:

Vosne Romanée
J. Confuron Cotetidot
Burgundy

Brunello
Bondi Santi
Tuscany

Barolo
Az. Agr. Pira e Figli
Piedmont

Guinea Hen in Chanterelle Sauce with Lemon–Lime Noodles

SERVES 4

3 oz (80 g) bacon, cut into strips

1 cup (250 mL) sliced chanterelles or other seasonal mushrooms

¾ cup (175 mL) pearl onions, peeled, about 20 onions

¼ cup (50 mL) flour

1 tbsp (15 mL) chopped fresh rosemary

½ tsp (2 mL) each, salt and pepper

4 guinea hen breasts

½ cup (125 mL) Madeira

2 tbsp (30 mL) cognac

1 cup (250 mL) game stock or chicken stock *(p. 100)*

1 tbsp (15 mL) chopped fresh chives

LEMON–LIME NOODLES:

pinch saffron

¼ cup (50 mL) hot water

2½ cups (375 mL) flour

⅓ cup (75 mL) semolina

1½ tbsp (20 mL) finely chopped lemon zest

2 tsp (10 mL) finely chopped lime zest

¼ tsp (1 mL) salt

1 egg, beaten

1 tbsp (15 mL) olive oil

In a large, deep skillet, over medium-high heat, cook bacon until well browned. Pour off all but 1 tbsp (15 mL) fat. Add chanterelles and pearl onions and sauté for 2–3 minutes, or until golden brown. Remove bacon and mushrooms from pan, leaving onions; reserve.

Place ½ the flour, rosemary, salt, and pepper in a plastic bag, and shake each breast until coated.

Using the same hot skillet, cook breasts, along with the onions, skin side down, for 10 minutes, turning once. Remove the breasts and the onions and set aside.

TO PREPARE THE LEMON–LIME NOODLES: Stir saffron into hot water. Let stand to cool. In a large bowl, stir together flour, semolina, lemon and lime zest, and salt. Make a well in flour mixture, and pour in water, egg, and olive oil. Stir to make a ragged dough. Turn dough out onto counter; knead for 2–3 minutes until smooth. Wrap in plastic wrap and let rest 30 minutes if using pasta maker, or 2 hours if rolling by hand.

For pasta-maker method, divide dough into 5 pieces; feed through lasagna press on medium setting. Stack sheets of pasta and slice into ¼-inch (8-mm) broad noodles. If rolling by hand, lightly dust counter with flour. Roll dough with a rolling pin, until very thin. Using a straight edge, slice into linguine noodles.

continued on P.92

In a large pot of boiling salted water, cook noodles for 3–4 minutes until cooked through. Double cooking time if noodles have been left to dry.

Pour the Madeira and cognac in the skillet, stirring for 1 minute. Add stock; whisk in remaining flour, and simmer for about 15 minutes, or until beginning to thicken. Return guinea hen, bacon, and mushrooms and onions to pan, until just heated through.

To serve: Garnish breasts with the chopped chives, and serve hot with lemon–lime egg noodles.

Chef's Suggestion: Chicken may be substituted for the guinea hen, in which case, return breasts to pan after whisking in the flour. Simmer for 20–25 minutes or until cooked through.

Veal Tenderloin with Ragoût of Leeks and Wild Mushrooms in Tarragon Sauce

S E R V E S 4

RECOMMENDED WINES:

Merlot
Bankcroft Ranch
Beringer
Napa Valley

Crozes-Hermitages
Mornay Sorreles
Rhône

Chianti Classico Il Picchio
Az. Agr. Castello di Querceto
Tuscany

1 cup (250 mL) brown chicken stock *(p. 100)*

2 tbsp (30 mL) fresh tarragon, finely chopped

2 cups (500 mL) julienned leeks

8 pieces veal tenderloin (3½ oz/ 80 g each)

1 tbsp (15 mL) extra virgin olive oil

½ cup (125 mL) finely chopped shallots

12 oyster mushrooms, cleaned

10 chanterelles, cleaned

16 black trumpet mushrooms, cleaned and halved

salt and pepper

In a saucepan over medium-high heat, reduce chicken stock by ½, and add tarragon. Reserve.

Blanch leeks for 30 seconds in boiling salted water. Plunge into ice water, and cool for 2 minutes. Drain thoroughly.

Season veal medallions with salt and pepper and sauté in a hot non-stick frying pan for 2–3 minutes. Remove to a warm platter, and tent with foil.

Using the same pan, sauté the chopped shallots in 1 tbsp (15 mL) oil until transparent; remove from pan, and reserve.

Add oyster, chanterelle, and black trumpet mushrooms to the same hot pan, and sauté for 1 minute. Stir in leeks, and cook, stirring constantly, for 1–2 minutes. Add shallots to the pan; season to taste with salt and pepper.

TO SERVE: Place equal amounts of ragoût in the centre of each of 4 dinner plates, and top each with 2 veal medallions. Pour tarragon sauce over the veal and around the ragoût.

RECOMMENDED WINES:

Darmagi
Angelo Gaja
Piedmont

Château Latour
Pauillac-Médoc
Bordeaux

Cabernet Sauvignon
Maestroraro
Fattoria di Felsina
Tuscany

Ontario Spring Lamb Tenderloin with Herb and Citrus Jus

SERVES 4

2 tbsp (30 mL) extra virgin olive oil
1 clove garlic, halved
1 sprig each, thyme and rosemary
8 lamb tenderloins
½ tsp (2 mL) each, salt and pepper

¾ cup (175 mL) lamb jus (*p. 103*)
½ tsp (2 mL) each, chopped fresh rosemary, parsley, thyme, and oregano
1 tsp (5 mL) mixed chopped lemon, lime, and orange zest

¼ cup (50 mL) butter, cut in cubes

In a shallow dish, combine olive oil, garlic, and thyme and rosemary sprigs; add tenderloins, and turn to coat in oil mixture. Cover, and refrigerate for 24 hours.

Remove meat from refrigerator 30 minutes before cooking and pour off excess oil into an ovenproof pan. Season meat with salt and pepper. Set pan over high heat, add tenderloins, and sear, turning often, for about 3 minutes, until well browned on all sides. Transfer pan to a 400 F (200 C) oven for 5 minutes, or until lamb is cooked to medium rare. Remove pan from oven, and transfer tenderloin to a heated platter; tent with foil, and let rest.

In a small saucepan, bring the lamb jus, rosemary, parsley, thyme, and oregano to a boil; simmer rapidly for 7–10 minutes, or until reduced to about ½ cup (125 mL). Stir in the zest. Reduce heat to low, and whisk in cubed butter, bit by bit. Keep warm.

TO SERVE: Cut, 2 tenderloins per person, on the diagonal, into thin strips. Arrange in a circular pattern on individual plates. Drizzle with jus.

infandel

Alcohol 13.5% by Volume

Niagara Peach Crème Brûlée

SERVES 6

2¼ cups (550 mL) 35% cream
2 vanilla beans, sliced lengthwise
5 egg yolks
¼ cup (50 mL) granulated sugar

1 large peach, poached and thinly
  sliced
½ cup (125 mL) granulated sugar

In a saucepan over medium heat, heat the cream and vanilla beans until steaming.

In a double boiler or large heat-proof bowl set over barely simmering water, whisk egg yolks and sugar for about 1 minute, or until mixture thickens. Slowly whisk hot cream into yolk mixture; remove vanilla beans. Cook mixture over a pot of barely simmering water for 40–45 minutes, whisking frequently, until it is thick enough to heavily coat the back of a spoon and does not readily drip off.

Divide slices of poached peach evenly among 6 heatproof dessert dishes or ramekins. Spoon in enough custard to cover fruit, leaving ⅛ inch (2.5 mm) space at the top.

Refrigerate for at least 1 hour until set.

TO CARAMELIZE: In a small saucepan over high heat, melt ½ cup (125 mL) sugar for 5–6 minutes, or until all crystals have disappeared and the sugar is a light caramel colour. Pour immediately onto aluminum foil, and cool. Once cooled, break into pieces, and powder in a food processor. Spoon sugar powder evenly over tops of custards; place under hot broiler for 20–30 seconds or until sugar dissolves and forms a hard coating. Return to refrigerator for 15 minutes to harden the caramel tops.

Fresh Berry Napoleon with Lemon Curd

SERVES 4

LEMON CURD:

2 eggs
2 egg yolks
¾ cup (175 mL) granulated sugar
1 cup (250 mL) lemon juice
½ cup (125 mL) finely chopped
    lemon zest
2 tbsp (30 mL) finely grated lime
    zest

HONEY WAFER CUPS:

2 tbsp (30 mL) softened butter
¼ cup (50 mL) confectioners'
    sugar
3 tbsp (45 mL) liquid honey
⅓ cup (75 mL) flour
pinch of anise powder

BERRIES:

6 cups (1.5 L) mixed fresh berries
    or fruits
2 tbsp (30 mL) Grand Marnier

TO PREPARE THE LEMON CURD: In the top of a double boiler or large heatproof bowl, whisk together eggs, egg yolks, sugar, lemon juice, and lemon and lime zest. Whisk over boiling water for 10 minutes until thick enough to mound. Remove from heat; cool to room temperature. Refrigerate for 20 minutes until thoroughly chilled and set.

TO PREPARE THE WAFER CUPS: In a small bowl, blend together butter, sugar, and honey. Stir in flour and anise powder; stir vigorously until well combined.

On lightly greased baking sheet, using back of a spoon, spread 1 tsp (5 ml) of batter into a 2½-inch (5.5-cm) circle. Repeat with remaining dough. Bake in 400 F (200 C) oven for about 3 minutes, or until cookies are evenly browned. Cool on baking sheet for 5 minutes; gently remove with metal spatula.

TO PREPARE THE BERRIES: In bowl, gently stir together berries/fruit and Grand Marnier.

TO ASSEMBLE: In the centre of each of 4 plates, create a Napoleon using 4 wafers per plate. Alternate wafer, lemon curd, and berries. Top the final wafer with some lemon curd. This may be sprinkled with granulated sugar and caramelized under a hot broiler if desired. Plate may be decorated with various fruit coulis.

Palate Cleansers

The chef has recommended a palate cleanser for each of the special seasonal menus. These are to be taken in the middle of a large meal to refresh the palate as well as to stimulate the appetite for the remaining courses.

Melon Consommé

Purée peeled chunks of 1 melon with 1/2 cup (125 mL) lemon juice in a food processor or blender; strain through a fine-mesh sieve; discard purée. Serve consommé over ice.

Champagne Sorbet

Serve two or three small balls of sorbet in a stemmed flute and cover with champagne.

Sorbet with Grappa or Marc

Marc, like Italian grappa, is distilled from the debris remaining after the final pressing of grapes for wine. Fruit sorbet sprinkled with marc is often substituted for the trou normand. A noted marc from Alsace is made from Gewüztraminer pressings.

Le Trou Normand

A small glass of spirits, traditionally Calvados, taken neat. The name refers to Normandy, where Calvados is distilled.

Stocks and Jus

All stocks and jus may be made in advance and refrigerated for up to 5 days. Allow stock to cool completely before covering. Many of the recipes allow chicken stock as an alternative for the convenience of home use; however, the restaurant would use the stock or jus appropriate for the recipe.

Chicken Stock

Yield 4 cups (1 L)
2 lb (1 kg) poultry bones, chopped
8 cups (2 L) water
1 onion, chopped
½ cup (125 mL) each, chopped leek (white only) and celery
1 bay leaf
1 sprig rosemary
salt and pepper

In a large pot, combine bones and water. Bring to a boil; reduce heat to medium low. Skim off foam. Stir in onion, leeks, celery, bay leaf, and rosemary, and simmer for 30 minutes, skimming frequently. Simmer 1 hour longer, or until reduced to about 4 cups (1 L). Strain through a fine sieve; lightly season with salt and pepper.

Brown Chicken Stock

Yield 4 cups (1 L)
2 lb (1 kg) poultry bones and trimmings, chopped
1 each onion and carrot, finely chopped
½ cup (125 mL) celery root, chopped
2 sprigs rosemary
1 tsp (5 mL) tomato paste
1 plum tomato, diced
8 cups (2 L) water

Preheat oven to 350 F (180 C), and roast bones and trimmings until brown, stirring occasionally. Add vegetables and rosemary; continue roasting for another 4–5 minutes. Drain off fat, and add tomato paste and diced tomato. Roast another 4–7 minutes. Remove roasting pan from oven, and transfer contents to a saucepan. Add 2 cups (500 mL) water, bring to a boil, and reduce to a glaze. Add another 2 cups (500 mL) water, and reduce again. Add remaining water; and simmer, uncovered, for 1 hour, periodically skimming and removing excess fat. Strain through a fine sieve.

Game Stock

Substitute trimmings and bones from appropriate game recipe and follow the recipe for Chicken Stock.

Fish Stock

Yield 4 cups (1 L)
¼ cup (50 mL) extra virgin olive oil
3 onions, chopped
½ fennel, chopped
1 clove garlic, halved

2 tomatoes, chopped
1 tbsp (15 mL) tomato paste
1 lb (500g) fish bones
2 cups (500 mL) white wine
4 cups (1L) water

Fish stock should be brought to a boil quickly, skimmed, and simmered for no longer than 40 minutes. The vegetables must be cut small so that they cook entirely in this short time.

Heat oil in a Dutch oven set over medium heat; add onions, fennel, and garlic. Cook, stirring often, for about 7 minutes, or until golden. Stir in tomatoes and tomato paste; increase heat to high, and cook, stirring, for 3 minutes. Add fish bones, and continue cooking for 2 minutes, until aromatic. Pour in wine and water; bring to a boil. Reduce heat to medium low; simmer for 30 minutes. Season to taste.

Remove from heat, let sit for 5 minutes, and carefully ladle all of the stock through a fine strainer into a clean pot. Discard the bones. Immediately refrigerate the stock, uncovered.

Beef Stock

Yield 8 cups (2 L)
2 tbsp (30 mL) vegetable oil
4 lb (2 kg) beef trimmings and bones
2 each, small onion, carrot, and celery stalks, chopped
8 cloves garlic, peeled and chopped
4 plum tomatoes, chopped

2 sprigs each, rosemary and thyme
16 cups (4 L) water
salt and pepper

In a roasting pan, stir together oil, trimmings, and bones; place in 400 F (200 C) oven for 30 minutes, until well browned. Drain off fat and stir in onion, carrot, celery, garlic, tomatoes, rosemary, and thyme. Roast for 10 minutes.

Transfer pan contents to stock pot or Dutch oven, making sure to scrape any pan bits into the pot. Add 4 cups (1 L) water to roasted mixture and bring to boil for about 15 minutes until reduced to 1 cup (250 mL). Stir in remaining water and gently simmer for 4–5 hours, skimming occasionally, or until stock is reduced to about 8 cups (2 L). Strain through a fine sieve; season with salt and pepper to taste. Chill and skim off excess fat.

Veal Stock

Substitute the trimmings and bones from the appropriate veal recipe and follow the recipe method for Beef Stock.

Game Jus

Yield ⅔ cups (150 mL)
2 lbs (1 kg) duck bones and trimmings
1 tbsp (15 mL) extra virgin olive oil
1 carrot, diced
1 small onion, diced
4 garlic cloves
1 sprig each, rosemary and thyme

6 juniper berries
1 tsp (5 mL) tomato paste
⅓ cup (75 mL) port
⅓ cup (75 mL) red wine
¼ cup (50 mL) cognac
4 cups (1 L) water
salt and pepper to taste

Preheat oven to 450 F (230 C). Roast duck bones and trimmings in a roasting pan with olive oil until brown. Remove pan from the oven, and strain off the fat. Add carrot, onion, garlic, herbs, and juniper berries, and return to the oven for another 10 minutes.

Add tomato paste, stir in with a wooden spoon, and roast for another 5 minutes. Remove pan from oven, and transfer the contents to a saucepan. Cook on high heat, deglaze the mixture with the port, red wine, and cognac. Reduce to ½ volume. Add water, and let simmer until reduced again to ½. Strain through cheesecloth or fine sieve and season with salt and pepper. For a stronger, more intense stock, reduce for a little longer.

Lobster Jus

Yield 3½ cups (750 mL)
¼ cup (50 mL) extra virgin olive oil
shells from two cooked lobsters
¼ cup (50 mL) cognac
1 cup (250 mL) shallots, finely chopped
¼ cup (50 mL) carrot, finely chopped
6 cloves garlic, chopped

2 cups (500 mL) dry white wine
4 cups (1 L) fish stock *(p. 100)*
1 cup (250 mL) water
1 tomato, chopped
1 tbsp (15 mL) tomato paste
1 tsp (5 mL) pink peppercorns
1 bay leaf
3 sprigs tarragon

Heat ½ the olive oil in a large deep frying pan over high heat. Add the lobster shells, and cook for 5 minutes, stirring occasionally. Add the cognac, and deglaze for 2 minutes, until reduced to 1 tbsp (15 mL).
In a stock pot, heat the remaining oil over medium heat. Sauté shallots, carrots, and garlic, and cook for about 5 minutes, until softened. Add the lobster-shell mixture; stir in the wine, bring to a boil, and simmer rapidly for 6–7 minutes to reduce to 1 cup (250 mL). Add the fish stock and water, and bring mixture back to a boil. Add tomato, tomato paste, peppercorns, bay leaf, and tarragon; reduce heat to low, and simmer for 25 minutes. Pass through a fine sieve or cheesecloth before use.

Veal Jus

Yield 2 cups (500 mL)
1 tbsp (15 mL) extra virgin olive oil
2 lb (1 kg) chopped veal trimmings and bones
3 onions, chopped
2 carrots, chopped
½ small celery root, chopped
2 tbsp (30 mL) tomato paste

8 cups (2 L) water

2 cups (500 mL) each, white wine and port

In a roasting pan, stir together oil and veal trimmings and bones until evenly coated. Roast in a 425 F (220 C) oven for 45 minutes, or until well browned. Stir in onions, carrots, and celery root. Continue roasting for 15 minutes. Drain off excess fat.

Stir in tomato paste, coating bones and vegetables evenly. Roast for about 10 minutes, until tomato paste is slightly browned. Transfer to a stock pot set over high heat. Stir in 2 cups (500 mL) water and bring to a boil for 15 minutes or until reduced to about ½ cup (125 mL). Stir in 2 additional cups (500 mL) water; simmer 15 minutes longer, until equally reduced. Add remaining water, wine, and port. Bring stock to a boil; reduce heat to medium low, and simmer gently for 1½–2 hours, skimming often. Strain through a fine sieve.

Lamb Jus

Yield 2 cups (500 mL)

2 lb (1 kg) lamb trimmings, or combination of
   bones/trimmings cut in small pieces

1 tbsp (15 mL) vegetable oil

1 each, small onion, carrot, and celery stalk,
   chopped

4 cloves garlic, peeled and chopped

2 plum tomatoes, diced

1 sprig each, rosemary and thyme

8 cups (2 L) water

pepper

In a roasting pan, stir together trimmings and oil. Place in 400 F (200 C) oven for 30 minutes, or until well browned. Drain off fat, and add the chopped vegetables, garlic, diced tomatoes, rosemary, and thyme; roast for another 10 minutes.

Transfer contents of roasting pan to a wide, shallow saucepan, scraping cooked-on pieces into the new pan. Add 2 cups (500 mL) water, and bring to a boil. Boil rapidly until reduced to about ½ cup (125 mL)—about 15 minutes. Stir in another 2 cups (500 mL) water, bring to a boil, and reduce again. Stir in the remaining 4 cups (1 L) water, and simmer until reduced by about ½, skimming occasionally—25–35 minutes. Jus will be glossy and thickened. Strain through a fine sieve, and season to taste with pepper.

Venison Jus/Squab Jus

Yield ⅔ cup (150 mL)

2 lbs (1 kg) raw venison and beef bones and
   trimmings, chopped

1 tbsp (15 mL) extra virgin olive oil

1 carrot, diced

1 small onion, diced

4 cloves garlic

1 sprig each, rosemary and thyme

6 juniper berries

2 tsp (10 mL) tomato paste

½ cup (125 mL) each, port and red wine

¼ cup (50 mL) cooking brandy

½ cups (875 mL) chicken stock *(p. 100)* or water

salt and pepper

Preheat oven to 450 F (230 C). Roast venison bones and trimmings in a roasting pan with olive oil until brown, or for about 10 minutes. Remove pan from oven and strain off the fat. Stir in carrot, onion, garlic, herbs, and juniper berries, and return to the oven to roast for another 10 minutes. With a wooden spoon, stir in tomato paste and cook for 5 minutes longer.

Remove pan from oven, and transfer the contents to a large saucepan. Cook on high heat for 30 seconds, or until the bottom of the pan is beginning to brown. Deglaze the mixture with the port, wine, and brandy, stirring often, for about 8 minutes, or until reduced to ½ cup (125 mL) of liquid.

Add chicken stock and let simmer for 12–15 minutes until glossy and thick enough to coat the back of a spoon. Strain through a fine sieve, and season with salt and pepper. Refrigerate jus for 4 hours; skim off excess fat before using. For a stronger, more intense sauce, reduce for a little longer.

Substitute squab bones for venison bones and trimmings and proceed as above.

Jus de Nage
Yield 3 cups (750 mL)
1 carrot, chopped
½ each, onion and leek, chopped
4 cloves garlic, peeled and sliced
½ lemon, sliced
½ tsp (2 mL) white peppercorns
1 bay leaf
¼ tsp (1 mL) anise seeds
1 ½ cup (375 mL) water
1 sprig each, parsley and coriander
¼ cup (50 mL) white wine

Place carrot, onion, leek, and garlic in a large saucepan with lemon, peppercorns, bay leaf, and anise seeds. Add enough water to cover, and bring to a boil. Reduce the heat, and allow to simmer for at least 10 minutes. Add the parsley and coriander, and simmer for 3 minutes longer. Remove the pan from the heat, and add the wine. Pour the whole mixture into a jar, cover, and let cool for 1 hour in the refrigerator.

Unlike other jus, Jus de Nage may be kept in a sterilized jar for up to 1 month in the refrigerator. This jus is excellent for poaching any fish or crustacean as well as an additional base for vegetable soup.

Stock Syrup – Simple Syrup
Yield 3 cups (750 mL)
2 cups (500 mL) granulated sugar
1 cup (250 mL) water

Dissolve the sugar in the water by bringing to a boil and stirring. Make sure all the sugar is dissolved; continue to boil the syrup for another 2 minutes.

Shopping Guide

This guide is by no means exhaustive. As many of these Toronto retailers have more than one outlet, and as they do not all carry the same stock, it is best to check with your nearest store. Certain items, such as foie gras, tripe, and fresh duck, should be ordered in advance. St. Lawrence Market and Kensington Market are good sources for some of the ingredients.

Fresh Truffles, Bottled Truffles, Truffle Oil, Champagne Vinegar, Caviar

All the Best Fine Foods
Dinah's Cupboard
Harvest Wagon
Pascale Gourmet
Pusateri's Fine Foods
Summerhill Market

Venison, Rabbit, Guinea Hens, Dungeness Crab, Foie Gras,

Bloor St. Meat Market
Bruno's Fine Foods
Cumbrae Butchers
Nortown
Ollife
Pusateri's Fine Foods
Mike's Fish

Mirin, Tamari, Buckwheat Flour

Pisces Gourmet
The Big Carrot

Tripe

Ferlisi Bros.
Bruno's Fine Foods

Armenian Flat Bread*

1 tsp (5 mL) dry active yeast
2½ cup (600 mL) cold water
¼ cup (50 mL) butter or
    shortening
2 whole eggs
3 tbsp (45 mL) sugar
1 tbsp (15 mL) salt
6 cups (1.5 L) flour

Mix all ingredients and knead as for bread dough. Use a mixer on the first speed, for 15-20 minutes. Divide the dough into 12 portions, or amounts of dough for the desired size sheets. Dough may be frozen at this point, and used when needed.

For immediate use, let portions rest for one hour. Roll out dough into large flat sheets to fit a cookie sheet; spray with water, and sprinkle with sesame or poppyseeds or herb of choice. Bake at 350F (180C), for 15 minutes.

see front jacket picture

Glossary

AL DENTE: Usually used in reference to pasta. Means slightly undercooked, offering a slight resistance when bitten.

BAIN MARIE: Similar to a double boiler. Used for cooking dishes very slowly. Prepared dishes can be kept warm in these containers until ready for service.

BOCCONCINI: Small nuggets of fresh mozzarella cheese packed in whey or water.

BOUQUET-GARNI: Often a mixture of 2 tsp (10 mL) each of parsley, thyme, and marjoram; ½ tsp (2 mL) whole black peppercorns; and 1 bay leaf—used to flavour meat and soup. Usually tied together in a small bundle in a cheesecloth pouch to prevent them from dispersing in the liquid and removed before serving.

CARAMELIZE: To heat sugar, or food containing sugar, until dark brown and melted; develops a particular buttery nut flavour.

CÈPES: Species of wild mushroom. Also referred to as "porcini."

CHANTERELLE: Trumpet-shaped wild mushroom. Because they tend to toughen when overcooked, it is best to add them towards the end of the cooking time.

CHAR or CHARR: Fish from icy waters; similar to trout and salmon in taste and texture.

COMPOTE: A combination of fresh or dried fruit cooked in a sugar syrup; served as a relish.

COULIS: A thick purée or sauce. Served as a flavour enhancer or an accompaniment.

COURT BOUILLON: A broth made by cooking various vegetables and herbs in water together with wine, lemon juice, or vinegar. Traditionally used for poaching fish or seafood, and occasionally white meat such as chicken and veal.

CROUSTILLANT: A thin, crispy layer of puff pastry that is used as a separating layer between alternate tastes. Similar to a Napoleon.

CURD: A creamy mixture made from citrus juice, sugar, butter, and egg yolks. When cool, it becomes thick enough to spread.

DARNE: A thick transverse slice of fish, such as hake, salmon, tuna, or large fresh water fish such as pike. The word comes from the Breton darn, meaning "piece." This cut may successfully be poached, braised, or grilled.

DEGLAZE: To dilute a roasting pan's juices with a liquid, usually wine or stock. Deglazing is done by heating a small amount of liquid in the pan and stirring to loosen browned bits of food on the pan bottom. Used as a base for a sauce to accompany the food cooked in the pan.

EMULSION: The binding together of two or more liquids not mutually soluble. Emulsifying is done by slowly adding one ingredient to another while simultaneously, mixing rapidly. When two liquids are thoroughly beaten together, one will divide into globules that will be completely surrounded by the other, as with butter, egg yolks, and lemon juice, as in mayonnaise.

ESCALOPE: A thin slice of meat or fish usually flattened. Requires very light cooking; often referred to as "scallop" or Italian "scaloppini."

ESSENCE: A concentrated aromatic liquid used to enhance certain culinary preparations; adds flavour to other foods.

FEUILLETÉ: A very crisp, light puff pastry consisting of paper-thin layers of dough; used when very light fluffy pastry is required. Also refers to small sticks of flaky pastry brushed with a little egg yolk and sprinkled with cumin seeds, cheeses, or paprika, and served hot as cocktail snacks.

FIVE-SPICE POWDER: Used extensively in Chinese cooking; a pungent mixture of five ground spices, usually cinnamon, cloves, fennel seeds, star anise, and Szechuan peppercorns. Prepackaged five-spice powder is available in Asian markets and most supermarkets.

FONDUE: In French cooking, refers to finely chopped vegetables that have been reduced to a pulp by lengthy and slow cooking. This mixture is often used as a garnish for meat or fish.

FOOD MILL: A kitchen utensil described as a "mechanical sieve." A hand-turned paddle forces food through a strainer plate, removing skin, seeds and fibre.

GANACHE: A flavoured cream made with chocolate, butter, and fresh cream, used to decorate desserts or fill cakes. It was created in Paris in 1850.

GNOCCHI: Italian dumplings made of potatoes, flour, or farina, in the shape of little oblong balls. Poached and served with butter or savoury sauce.

GRAPESEED OIL: Extract from grape seeds which has a light grapey flavour and fragrance. Excellent for salad dressings, and has a very high smoke point, which makes it well suited for use in sautéing.

INFUSION: Liquid impregnated with the essence of a solid by steeping, i.e., tea, coffee.

JUS DE NAGE: A light white wine–based vegetable stock, in which scallops and small crustaceans may be poached. The name literally means "swimming." May also be used as a base for vegetable soup.

LANGOUSTINE: A delicate shellfish with very sweet meat that tastes like a cross between lobster and shrimp.

LEMON GRASS: A scented grass used as a herb in Southeast Asian cooking. Usually the outer leaves are removed and only the bottom third of the stalk is used. Has a lemony-strawlike flavour.

LOLLO ROSSO: A delicate leafy lettuce used in salad.

MARINADE: An acidic aromatic liquid used to flavour food, and also to make certain meats more tender by softening the fibres.

MASCARPONE CHEESE: A buttery-rich double or triple-cream cheese made from cow's milk. From the Lombard region of Italy.

MESCLUN GREENS: A mixture of red oak leaf, arugula, frisée, and other small-leaf lettuces.

MILLE-FEUILLE: "A thousand leaves." This classic dessert is two layers of puff pastry spread with cream or custard, jam, or fruit purée; dusted with sugar or decorated with fruit. For the recipe in this book, the term is used to describe the layering approach of the presentation, i.e., potato crisps instead of puff pastry are used as the separating layers.

MIREPOIX: A mixture of diced onions, carrots, celery, and peppers sautéed slowly in butter; used to season other preparations.

MIRIN: A sweet, golden wine made from glutinous rice; may be referred to as "rice wine" as it contains a trace of alcohol.

MOREL: Wild mushroom belonging to the same species as the truffle. Distinguishable by its honey-combed, cone-shaped cap, and its smoky, nutty flavour, applauded by gourmets.

PISTOU: A condiment made of fresh basil crushed with garlic and olive oil; sometimes supplemented by Parmesan cheese and tomatoes. Very similar to Italian pesto.

POLENTA: Cornmeal porridge; a traditional basic dish of northern Italy.

PORCINI: A species of mushroom; often referred to as "cèpe."

QUENELLE: A light, delicate dumpling made of seasoned minced or ground fish, meat, or vegetables bound with eggs and poached in stock. The term is used to describe a typical oval shape formed using two spoons.

RAGOÛT: A stew made from meat, poultry, fish, or vegetables cut into uniform pieces and cooked in a thickened liquid flavoured with herbs and seasonings. The French word is used to describe anything that stimulates the appetite or, figuratively, "awakes interest."

ROUILLE: A fiery-flavoured rust-coloured sauce, traditionally from Provence. It is served as a garnish with fish and fish stews such as bouillabaisse.

SEMOLINA: Grain, such as hard durham wheat, ground into granules. White semolina is ground from rice; semolina for polenta is ground from corn. Yellow semolina is made from wheat and coloured with saffron to resemble cornmeal.

SPECK: A fatty back bacon, cured by salting and also by smoking. In the Tyrol, apple wood smoking is most common.

SUPRÊME: "Best," "most delicate." The name given to breast and wing of chicken or game may also refer to a fine fillet of fish.

TAMARI: A gourmet soy sauce, may be substituted by other premium soy sauce.

TATAKI: A preparation method found in Japanese and Chinese cuisine, similar to that used in making gravlax. Refers to weighting down or twist-wrapping very tightly while marinating. This traditional time-consuming method has been simplified in the recipes for Trio of Tataki Marc Thuet and Tataki of Atlantic Salmon.

TÊTE-DE-MOINE CHEESE: A Swiss cow's milk cheese. Pressed and uncooked, it is a firm yet pliable cheese with a washed brownish-yellow rind. Has a spicy flavour and a pronounced aroma.

TIAN: An earthenware oven-proof dish from Provence. With slightly raised edges, it is used to prepare all kinds of gratin dishes called "tians," most commonly vegetables. In this book the term "tian" is used to describe a tiered effect created by layering ratatouille of vegetables with scallops and spinach.

TOURNEDO: A small round slice, ¾ inch (2 cm) thick and 2 inches (5 cm) in diameter, usually of beef. In the recipe for Croustillants Mille-feuilles of Foie Gras and Salmon, the term refers to the size and shape of the salmon and foie gras preparation.

TRIPE: The lining of the stomach of cows, pigs, and lambs; sold specially prepared and cleaned for cooking, or ready-cooked or pickled. Requires long slow cooking to break down tough fibre.

TRUFFLES: Black fungus-like mushrooms that grow underground only in certain regions of France or Italy. White truffles are much rarer and more expensive than the black.

Biographies

Prevedellos

Franco and Barbara Prevedello have worked side by side since the 1970s in Toronto, together creating and managing several of the city's trend-setting and flourishing restaurants.

Biffi Bistro, an innovative open-kitchen eatery that accompanied its exciting menu with boutique wines from Italy, was the first of the Prevedellos' creations. Biffi's immediate popularity led them to open Pronto Ristorante one year later, right across the street. During this hectic period, Barbara and Franco would pass each other crossing Mt. Pleasant Road, often exchanging necessary information in the middle of the street.

In 1987, when Biffi Bistro and Pronto Ristorante were in the capable hands of new operators, the Prevedellos devoted their energies to a new and larger operation, Centro Grill and Wine Bar. For years, Barbara was the first one to arrive at the restaurant in the morning, and Franco was the last one to leave at night. Although the Prevedellos' partnership has seen them through nine restaurant openings, it rarely leads to an agreement on what to have for dinner. For them, "Marriage is not merely sharing the fettuccine, but sharing the burden of finding the fettuccine restaurant in the first place."

Marc Thuet

Marc Thuet was born in Alsace, France, and is a fourth generation *chef de cuisine*. At the age of twelve, Marc was already familiar with the inside of a restaurant kitchen, helping his uncle in the family business after school.

Marc attained his degree in Culinary Management at the Lycée Hôtelier in Strasbourg, France, and worked in several Michelin-rated restaurants and hotels throughout Europe. Under the direction of master chef, Anton Mosimann, at the Dorchester Hotel in London, Marc witnessed and contributed to the development of *Cuisine naturelle*, the low-fat, low-cholesterol style of food preparation that is valued throughout the culinary world today.

In 1984, Marc immigrated to Canada to work at the Chateauneuf Restaurant of the then Hilton Harbour Castle Hotel. Before coming to Centro in 1990, he was at Three Small Rooms and the Courtyard Café at the Windsor Arms Hotel, where he worked with Michael Bonacini.

Marc has contributed recipes to the *Niagara Estate Winery Cookbook*, as well as to a special edition of the *Canadian Living Cookbook*.

Tony Longo

Tony was born in Toronto. As his family's business was in the wholesale fruit and vegetable market, Tony was exposed to the workings of the restaurant business when he was very young. He has been in the service industry since he was thirteen, and worked for several of the finest hotels and restaurants in Toronto.

His passion for wine has taken him to California, often for months at a time, to learn from the master vintners, and to experience the techniques of wine making. Tony came to Centro in 1988 and has contributed to the high standard of service that is synonymous with Centro Grill and Wine Bar. Working closely with Franco Prevedello, as captain and general manager, Tony became a partner in 1994.

This book was set in
Minion and Fenice typefaces
in QuarkXPress on an
Apple Macintosh computer.

Colour separations by
Rainbow Graphics, Hong Kong

Printed and bound in China by
Book Art Inc. Toronto